Jimmy & Nath are best mates who love making big, fun and outlandish radio shows. From weeknights broadcasting around Australia on the Hit Network to the Sydney breakfast show on 2DayFM, the boys have conquered radio in a plethora of slots and are followed by hundreds of thousands of listeners internationally.

They are known everywhere for the memorable content they burn into the brains of their audience, including the hugely successful Dad Jokes segment featuring gags from their famous friends and devoted listeners. Many of the best are in this book!

Jimmy & Nath have spent over ten years bringing laugh-out-loud content to listeners and going on wild, unpredictable adventures. (In other words, they're a boss's worst nightmare, but they say sorry afterwards, so it's all okay . . . #AskForgivenessNotPermission.) Loved by all, their shows delight a variety of audiences, from your five-year-old son to your eighty-year-old grandma.*

For proof please contact Nath's Nanny Lynne who can verify that grandmothers love Jimmy & Nath.

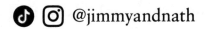 @jimmyandnath

Praise for

FUNNY STUFF NO ONE ASKED FOR

'I received my copy of the book early and I have not been able to leave the hospital because I have been in stitches ever since.'

Tones and I (one of Australia's most-streamed artists/Grammy nominee/obsessed with Jimmy & Nath)

'This book absolutely f#%&s just like Jimmy & Nath do!'

Teddy Swims (singer/super-sexy mother f#%£er)

'I don't even, like, read books, because that's hard. But if it's a book full of jokes I could read that, and like, I will buy this book and I will read it. Cause I think that's a fun time and an easy read.'

Meghan Trainor (Grammy-winning singer-songwriter)

'Run now for this book. Get it before it goes. And buy your own book, don't read anyone else's!'

Jessica Mauboy (singer/one of the loveliest humans on the planet/Australia's sweetheart)

'These two men that I met on a five-minute Zoom, everybody buy their book because they're hilarious.'

Jojo Siwa (singer/dancing sensation)

'Yeah they are pretty funny, these guys . . . so stop reading this and buy the book.'

Amy Shark (singer/songwriter/incredible parker of cars)

'Your shit has me laughing out loud, congrats boys on always cracking me up!'

Mark Cuban (businessman/film producer/TV personality)

'What, Harry Styles and Rihanna bought it? Omg Kim K loves it . . . it's the funniest thing I've ever read, so funny.'

'I would love to read that book.'

'When I first met y'all I felt like I had known you for years—your book better be better than how you play cornhole, can't wait to play again!'

FUNNY STUFF NO ONE ASKED FOR

Jimmy Smith & Nath Roye

ALLEN&UNWIN

SYDNEY • MELBOURNE • AUCKLAND • LONDON

First published in 2024

Allen & Unwin
Cammeraygal Country
83 Alexander Street
Crows Nest NSW 2065
Australia
Phone: (61 2) 8425 0100
Email: info@allenandunwin.com
Web: www.allenandunwin.com

*Allen & Unwin acknowledges the Traditional Owners of the Country on which we
live and work. We pay our respects to all Aboriginal and Torres Strait Islander
Elders, past and present.*

A catalogue record for this
book is available from the
National Library of Australia

NATIONAL
LIBRARY
OF AUSTRALIA

ISBN 978 1 76147 181 0

Internal design: Design by Committee
Set in 13.5/18 pt Sabon LT Pro by Bookhouse, Sydney
Printed and bound in Australia by the Opus Group

10 9 8 7 6 5 4 3 2 1

FOREWORD

Hello, soon-to-be readers of this book!

Firstly, stop reading right now if you aren't going to buy this. No freeloaders! Cheapskates . . .

Jimmy & Nath here, hi! We have a national radio show in Australia and we wanted to give special mention to our hilarious community of listeners and followers who have shared in the joy and helped us create this book; this one's dedicated to you. Together you have given us so many laughs and incredible stories that we now get to share with the world in book form.

Thank you all for being a part of the Jimmy & Nath family and we promise that within these pages will be many laughs. And if you find yourself offended by something, remember one simple thing: it's a joke, and the beauty of a book is you can turn the page . . . unless of course you get offended by a lot of things, in which case you might have to turn a few pages. Please don't get a paper cut.

Enough from us . . . now go get into the good stuff!

Jimmy & Nath x

CONTENTS

WORDPLAY WONDERS

Wordplay, puns and double entendres

The other day a girl asked me if I preferred breast or thigh. I said I'm more of an ass man. Then I got kicked out of KFC.

Anthony from Kilmore

My girlfriend has been asking me to blow on her at night. I'm not a fan.

Bec from Southport

What did the bra say to the hat?
You go on ahead, I'll give these two a lift.

Mick from Stroud

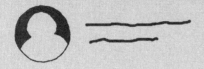

I bought a locket and put my own picture in it. Guess I really am . . . independent.

Jack from Glenelg

The population of Ireland's capital city is really growing . . . In fact it's Dublin.

Emily from Fannie Bay

What did the N say to the Z?
Get up bro, let's go.

Oliver from Stuart Park

Why was the broom late to work?
It overswept.

Noah from Deakin

Why do pirates never finish the alphabet?
Because they always get lost at C.

Damien from the Blue Mountains

Did you hear about the guy who drank
the invisible ink?
He's now in hospital waiting to be seen.

Chris from Canberra

The guy who stole my diary died yesterday.
My thoughts are with his family.

Zack from Bronte

Why do most bald people still own a
comb? They just can't part with it.

Courtney from Sandy Bay

I recently paid $1 for a wig . . .
It was a small price toupee.

Mo from Revesby

What do you call a man with a
rubber toe?
Roberto.

Helen from Sandgate

I've got this terrible disease where I can't
stop telling airport jokes . . .
My doctor says it's terminal.

Ardie from Runaway Bay

You're Australian when you go into the
bathroom and come out of it.
What are you when you are in it?
European (you're-a-peeing).

Stephanie from Gillieston Heights

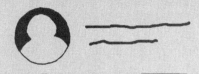

Why did the scarecrow get a promotion?
He was out standing in his field.

Anthony from Kilmore

Did you hear about the contortionist who
tried to fit into a colander?
He strained a muscle.

Anthony from Kilmore

What do you call someone with a shovel?
Doug.
What do you call a man without a shovel?
Dougless.

Tim from Canberra

Who can drink 20 litres of fuel?
Jerry can.

Kristy from Coffs Harbour

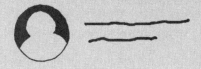

•••

What do you call a man in the ocean with
no arms and no legs?
Bob.

Jodie from Forster

Did you hear about the guy who
embroidered his initials on his balls?
Sew nuts.

Theo from Glenorchy

What did the o say to the q?
Dude, your dick's hanging out.

Stan from Dubbo

What did one door say to the other door?
Pull up your pants, I can see your knob.

Luke from Hobart

A man goes to a funeral and asks the
widow: mind if I say a word? She says:
please do. The man clears his throat and
says plethora. The widow replies: thanks,
that means a lot.

Anthony from Kilmore

I had to change my email password and I
tried the word fortnight.
But it said it was two week.

Jake from Warrane

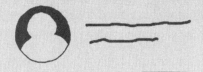

My partner asked me if I could clear the kitchen table . . . I needed a running start, but I just about managed it.

Anthony from Kilmore

I've been learning to speak German.
Do you know the word for virgin?
Goodentight.

Anthony from Kilmore

WORK WOES

Professions, occupations and general workplace banter

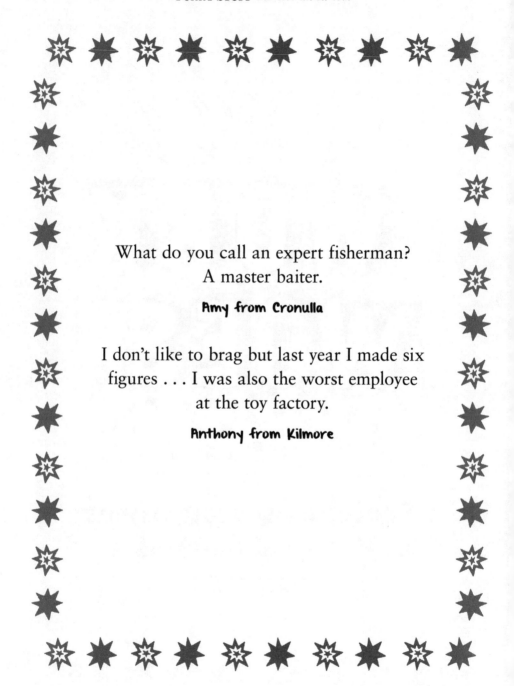

What do you call an expert fisherman?
A master baiter.

Amy from Cronulla

I don't like to brag but last year I made six
figures . . . I was also the worst employee
at the toy factory.

Anthony from Kilmore

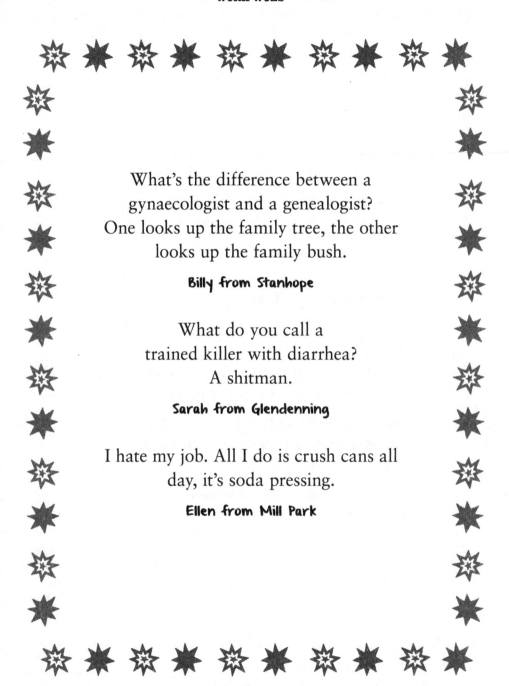

What's the difference between a
gynaecologist and a genealogist?
One looks up the family tree, the other
looks up the family bush.

Billy from Stanhope

What do you call a
trained killer with diarrhea?
A shitman.

Sarah from Glendenning

I hate my job. All I do is crush cans all
day, it's soda pressing.

Ellen from Mill Park

I got fired from my job at the bank. An old man came in and asked me to check his balance, so I pushed him over.

Rach from Newcastle

→ **Speaking of being** *fired, Nath once got fired by his own mother. She was the manager of a furniture store, and apparently turning up hungover and falling asleep for hours on the display mattresses wasn't the behaviour she was looking for in a junior warehouse manager (this was a self-appointed title, and one she refused to use). Safe to say it was an awkward family dinner that night.*

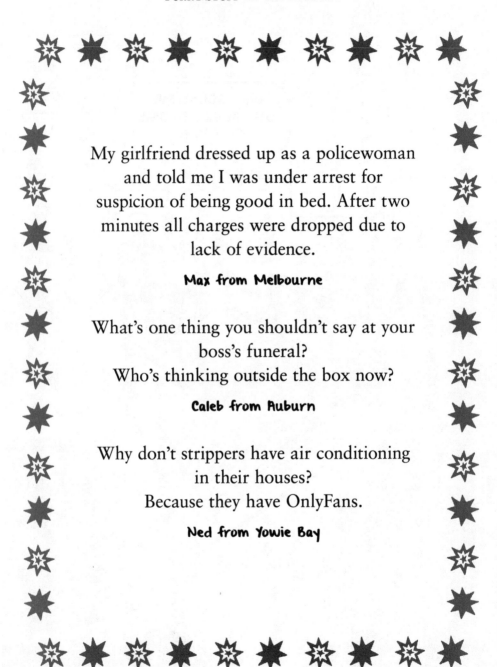

My girlfriend dressed up as a policewoman and told me I was under arrest for suspicion of being good in bed. After two minutes all charges were dropped due to lack of evidence.

Max from Melbourne

What's one thing you shouldn't say at your boss's funeral?
Who's thinking outside the box now?

Caleb from Auburn

Why don't strippers have air conditioning in their houses?
Because they have OnlyFans.

Ned from Yowie Bay

My dad always said, no news is good
news. Great guy, awful journalist.

Wayne from Red Hill

I quit my job at the helium factory today.
I refuse to be spoken to in that
tone of voice.

Joline from Newmarket

Why don't mummies take time off work?
Because they're afraid to unwind.

Lester from Wacol

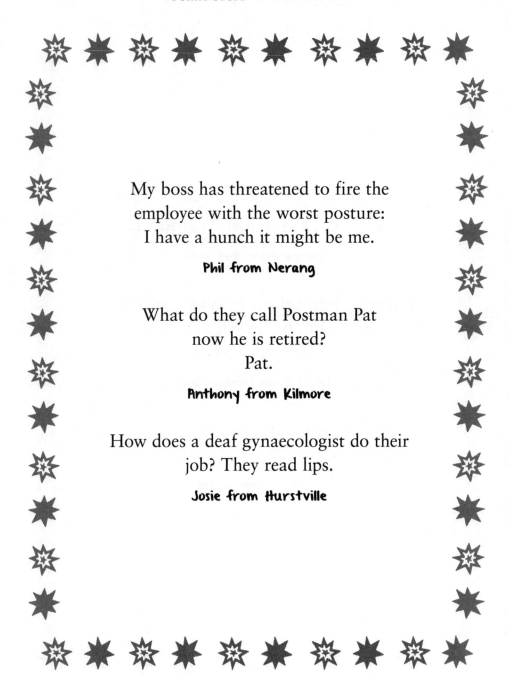

My boss has threatened to fire the
employee with the worst posture:
I have a hunch it might be me.

Phil from Nerang

What do they call Postman Pat
now he is retired?
Pat.

Anthony from Kilmore

How does a deaf gynaecologist do their
job? They read lips.

Josie from Hurstville

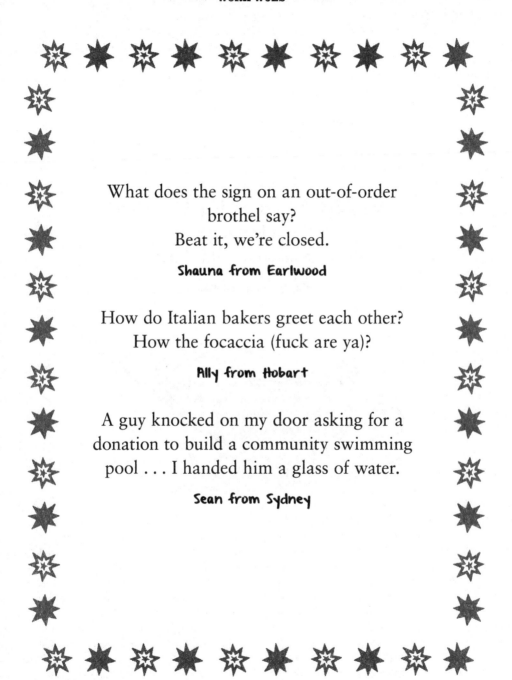

What does the sign on an out-of-order
brothel say?
Beat it, we're closed.

Shauna from Earlwood

How do Italian bakers greet each other?
How the focaccia (fuck are ya)?

Ally from Hobart

A guy knocked on my door asking for a
donation to build a community swimming
pool ... I handed him a glass of water.

Sean from Sydney

Why did the farmer drag his pig on
a leash?
He wanted some pulled pork.

Hank from Bayside

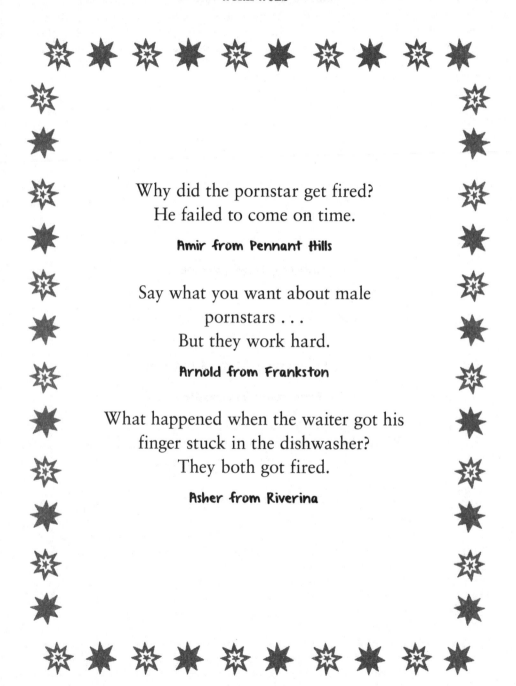

Why did the pornstar get fired?
He failed to come on time.

Amir from Pennant Hills

Say what you want about male
pornstars . . .
But they work hard.

Arnold from Frankston

What happened when the waiter got his
finger stuck in the dishwasher?
They both got fired.

Asher from Riverina

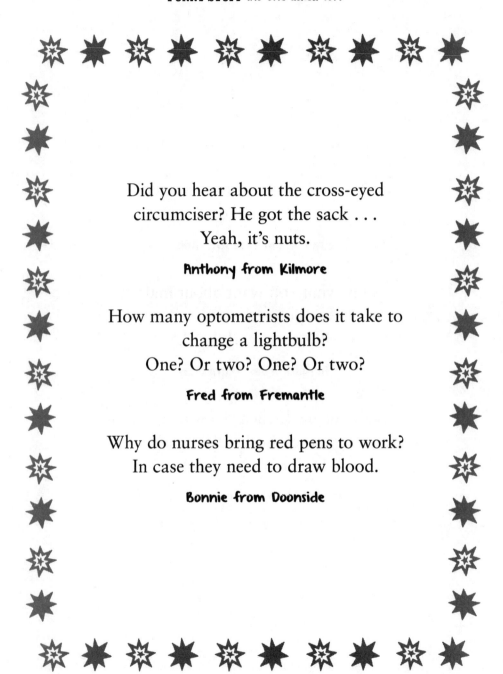

Did you hear about the cross-eyed
circumciser? He got the sack . . .
Yeah, it's nuts.

Anthony from Kilmore

How many optometrists does it take to
change a lightbulb?
One? Or two? One? Or two?

Fred from Fremantle

Why do nurses bring red pens to work?
In case they need to draw blood.

Bonnie from Doonside

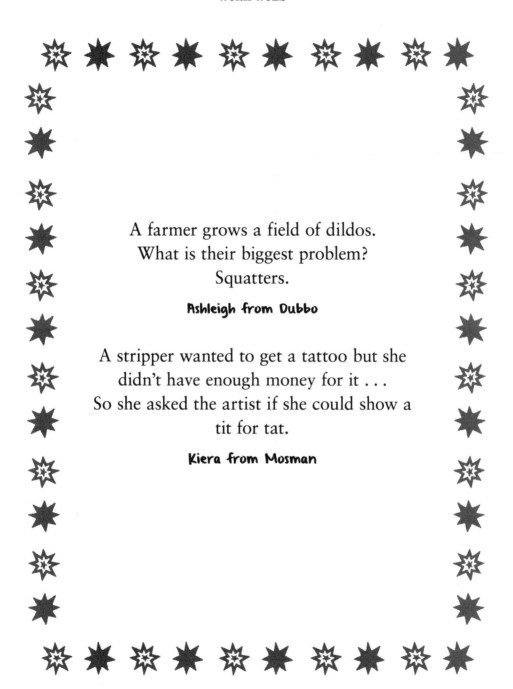

A farmer grows a field of dildos.
What is their biggest problem?
Squatters.

Ashleigh from Dubbo

A stripper wanted to get a tattoo but she
didn't have enough money for it . . .
So she asked the artist if she could show a
tit for tat.

Kiera from Mosman

I asked my surgeon if I could administer
my own anaesthetic . . .
He said sure, knock yourself out.

Jenny from Moonah

How come so many archaeologists are
women? Because they are very good at
digging up the past.

Kyle from Cronulla

What's the difference between a pickpocket and a peeping Tom? One snatches your watch, the other watches your snatch.

Aaron from Fremantle

A friend of mine got a girl pregnant without penetration . . . I would ask him for the story but he usually beats around the bush.

Anthony from Kilmore

I just came into a bunch of money . . . Which is strange for me because I usually just use tissues.

Elias from Diamond Creek

I arranged a threesome on the weekend . . .
Had two no-shows but still had fun.

Ethan from South Yarra

What do you call a person with erectile
dysfunction? It doesn't matter what you
call them; they're not going to come.

Emily from Ingleburn

What could you say during sex but also at
a family dinner?
Don't talk with your mouth full.

Noah from Sandy Bay

What do you call a man
with a small penis?
Just-in.

Phoebe from Rockdale

What comes after 69?
Mouthwash.

Melissa from Gymea

What's the difference between
light and hard?
I can't sleep with a light on.

Anthony from Kilmore

Why did the condom hit the roof?
Because it was pissed off.

Kim from Doreen

How do you cancel your appointment at
the sperm bank?
Tell them you can't come.

Jacob from Wagga Wagga

I think I've got a fetish for the last
paragraph in an essay . . .
I just came to that conclusion.

Jeremy from Victoria

Why did the walrus go to the
Tupperware party?
To find himself a tight seal.

Tom from Swan Hill

What did the penis say to the condom?
Cover me, I'm going in.

Mia from Hume

Which came first? The chicken or the egg?
Neither, the rooster did.

Anthony from Kilmore

Why did the snowman suddenly smile?
Because he saw the snow blower coming.

Gianna from Port Phillip

What has 38 teeth and
holds back the hulk?
My zipper.

Anthony from Kilmore

What did the barman say when five
penises walked into his bar?
You've got a lot of balls coming in here.
Why the schlong faces?

Ella from Dandenong

What has a hundred balls and
screws old women?
Bingo.

Douglas from Cremorne

How do you spot a blind guy
at a nudist beach?
It's not hard.

Shauna from Earlwood

What's the difference between having sex
in a canoe and light beer?
Nothing, they are both fucking near water.

Elias from North Adelaide

What goes in hard and dry
but comes out soft and wet?
Gum.

Ezra from Kensington

Two men broke into a pharmacy and stole all the Viagra. The police put out an alert for two hardened criminals.

Lucas from Coalcliff

What do you call a man
with a giant penis?
Phil.

Phil from Mornington

I used to be a porn addict.
It was the hardest time of my life.

Eli from Darwin

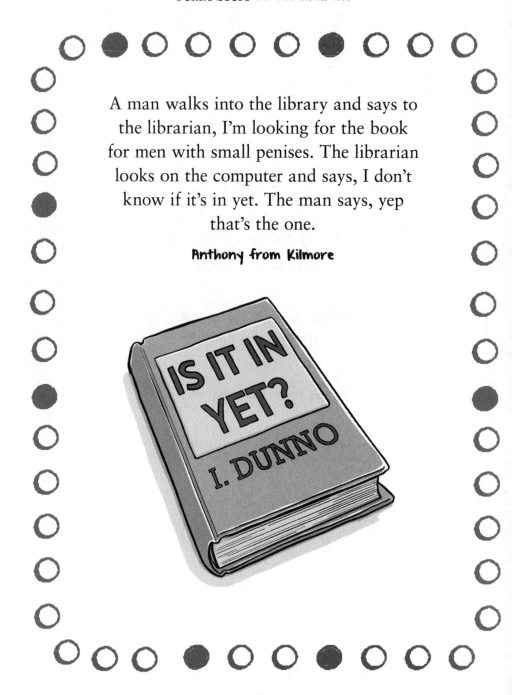

A man walks into the library and says to the librarian, I'm looking for the book for men with small penises. The librarian looks on the computer and says, I don't know if it's in yet. The man says, yep that's the one.

Anthony from Kilmore

I joined a fisting club recently. It's not something I'm particularly into, I'm just trying to widen the circle of my friends.

Kelly from Brighton

Why do I only let nerds buy me olive oil? Because I want it extra virgin.

Rach from Claremont

I don't know if tampons are the best invention ever but they are definitely up there.

Denny from the Gold Coast

I recently joined a nudist colony.
The first few days were the hardest.

Anthony from Kilmore

A guy walks into a bar and orders ten
shots of tequila. He seems normal enough,
so the bartender pours them. The guy does
his ten shots. 'What's the occasion?' asks
the bartender. 'First blow job,' says the
guy. 'Hey congratulations, have another
shot for free,' says the bartender.
'If the first ten didn't kill the taste, not
sure the eleventh will help.'

Mon from Adelaide

I asked my wife to let me know next time
she has an orgasm. She said she doesn't
like to bother me at work.

Anthony from Kilmore

HA HA HANIMALS

Animals and
animal-related
scenarios

Why do squirrels swim on their backs?
To keep their nuts dry.

Adrian from Bondi

What do you call a bird that
drinks too much?
An owlcoholic.

Steph from Marrickville

How does a penguin build its house?
Igloos it together.

Tahlia from Manly

What's the difference between
a piano and a fish?
You can tune a piano but you can't
tuna fish.

Eli from Tooradin

Male bees have a pretty sad life.
Honey. Nut. Cheerio.

Blake from Frankston

Why did the bird go to the gym?
To work on its pecks.

Sarah from Glendenning

What do you call a bee
that comes from America?
A USB.

Charlotte from Norwood

What happens when you have sex with a
cow and no one catches you?
So far nothing . . .

Anthony from Kilmore

If the dove is the bird of peace,
what is the bird of love?
The swallow.

Anthony from Kilmore

How do you circumcise a whale?
With four skin divers.

Anthony from Kilmore

Why don't they use female cows for meat?
Because that would be a huge miss-steak.

Enrique from Burwood

I recently took my chameleon to the vet.
He's waiting to be seen.

Kristy from Sydney

What do a dog and a narcissist have in
common? They both come to their name.

Leanne from Cranbourne East

What do you call a pig that does karate?
A pork chop.

Micheal from Mill Park

What do you call two monkeys
that share an Amazon account?
Prime mates.

Lisa from Gymea

Why do dogs float on water so well?
Because they are good buoys.

Josh from Bondi

What do you call a cow in an earthquake?
A milkshake.

Emily from Ingleburn

I caught my dog chewing on electrical
cords . . .
He's doing better now and
conducting himself properly.

Chantelle from Highgate

Why don't birds wear underwear?
Because their peckers are on their heads.

Vish from Ramsgate

What did the hammerhead shark say to his
buddies when he got laid?
Nailed it.

Kirby from Windsor

What do you get when you put brown
chickens and brown cows together?
Brown chicken brown cow (bow chicka
wow wow).

Tommo from Tumbi Umbi

Two cows are standing in a field. One cow
looks at the other and says,
'Moo,' and the other cow says, 'Fuck,
I was just about to say that.'

Kylie from the Central Coast

I can't take my dog to the park anymore.
The ducks keep biting him. I should have
known this would happen . . .
He is pure bread.

Ian from Pacific Pines

Why do ducks have tail feathers?
To cover their butt quacks.

Scott from Greensborough

What do you call a dear with no eyes?
No eye dear.

Allan from Albury

And what do you call a deer with no eyes
and no feet? Still no eye deer.

Eleanor from Lane Cove

Did you know that before the invention of crowbars, most crows drank at home?

Michael from Ascot Vale

→ **Speaking of home,** *Nath once tried to run away from home. It did not end well. He was five years old and had been sent to his room, so he decided to leg it to his grandmother's house a few streets away. He packed a bag with his teddy, a random bible (his family wasn't religious) and, ironically, a picture of his mum and dad. He opened his bedroom window and forgot that he was on the second level. So he fell out of the window, broke his ankle and started crying on the driveway, surrounded by everything in his bag. His parents found him there, took him to hospital and bought him ice-cream; it was the most successful running-away attempt that has ever happened.*

What do you get when you cross an
elephant with a rhino?
Elephino (el-if-I-know).

Alex from Toronto

What sort of bee produces milk?
A boobee.

Steve from Pakenham

What did the duck say
when buying ChapStick?
Put it on my bill.

Lilly from Maitland

Did you hear about the pregnant bed bug?
She gave birth in the spring.

Luke from Cardinia

Why do fish always know
how much they weigh?
Because they have their own scales.

Greg from Albury

Did you hear about the whale who
experiences pain during ejaculation?
Apparently it comes in waves.

Taylor from NSW

What's grey and comes in pints?
An elephant.

Anthony from Kilmore

I just got a pet termite and named it Clint,
Clint Eatswood.

Lincoln from Sydney

What do you call a seagull that
flies over a bay?
A bagel.

Bianca from Heathcote

What do you call a herd of masturbating cows? Beef stroganoff (stroking off).

Candice from Rutherford

Why was the horse named Mayo?
Because Mayo neighs.

Katherine from Adelaide

Why did the chicken cross
the basketball court?
Because the referee called a fowl.

Jason from Hobart

What's the best kind of music
to listen to when fishing?
Something catchy.

Hamish from Adelaide

My rescue dog has no legs,
so I named her Cigarette . . .
And every night we go for a drag.

April from Sydney

Why did Piglet have his head in the toilet?
He was looking for Pooh.

Chelsea from Melbourne

What do you call a rabbit
that picks its nose?
Boogs Bunny.

Carol from Blacktown

PICK-UP LINES YOU SHOULD NEVER USE

Are you as beautiful on the inside . . .
As you are on the outside?

Mike from Cabramatta

Are you a golf course?
Because I want to play all your holes.

Ben from Hobart

If you were a booger, I'd pick you first.

Cam from Adelaide

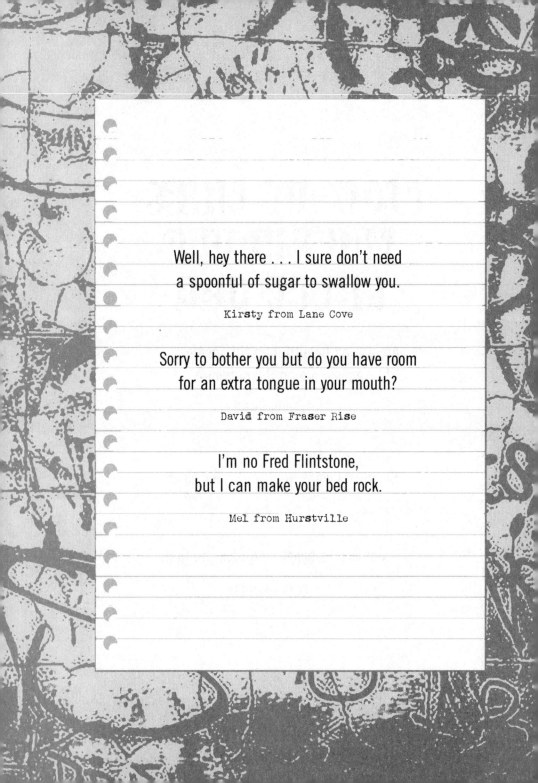

Well, hey there . . . I sure don't need
a spoonful of sugar to swallow you.

Kirsty from Lane Cove

Sorry to bother you but do you have room
for an extra tongue in your mouth?

David from Fraser Rise

I'm no Fred Flintstone,
but I can make your bed rock.

Mel from Hurstville

Are you a supermarket sample?
Because I want to taste you again and again
with no shame.

Stines from Parramatta

Let's play a game . . .
The fastest person to take off their clothes wins.

Lachy from Drummoyne

Are you an iceberg?
Because you are making me want to go down.

Raf from Jindabyne

What's the difference between
a Ferrari and an erection?
I don't have a Ferrari.

Blake from Frankston

I'm just like a pore strip:
it's hard to get me off but you'll be
extremely satisfied once you do.

Georgie from Corowa

I went to the doctor this morning and it turns out
I have a lack of vitamin D, would you like
to come back to my place and fix that?

Julie from Valla

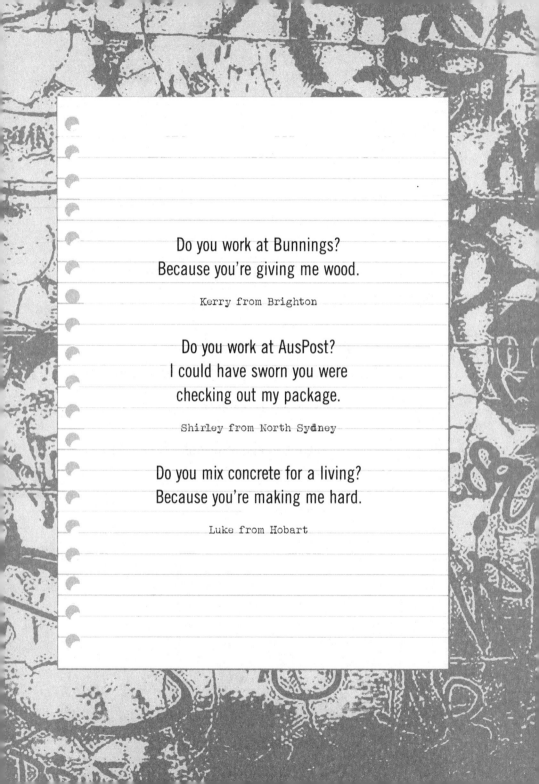

Do you work at Bunnings?
Because you're giving me wood.

Kerry from Brighton

Do you work at AusPost?
I could have sworn you were
checking out my package.

Shirley from North Sydney

Do you mix concrete for a living?
Because you're making me hard.

Luke from Hobart

If you were a doughnut, I'd jam ya.

Lexi from Heidelberg

Are your jeans made by Guess?
Because guess who wants to get in your pants?

Julie from Valla

I want to kiss your lips.
And the ones on your face.

Nathan from Thrumster

Is that a keg in your pants?
Because I'd love to tap that ass.

Eric from Liverpool

You can call me cake . . .
Because I'll go straight to that ass.

Sue from Goondiwindi

Let's only let latex stand between us.

Steve from Sydney

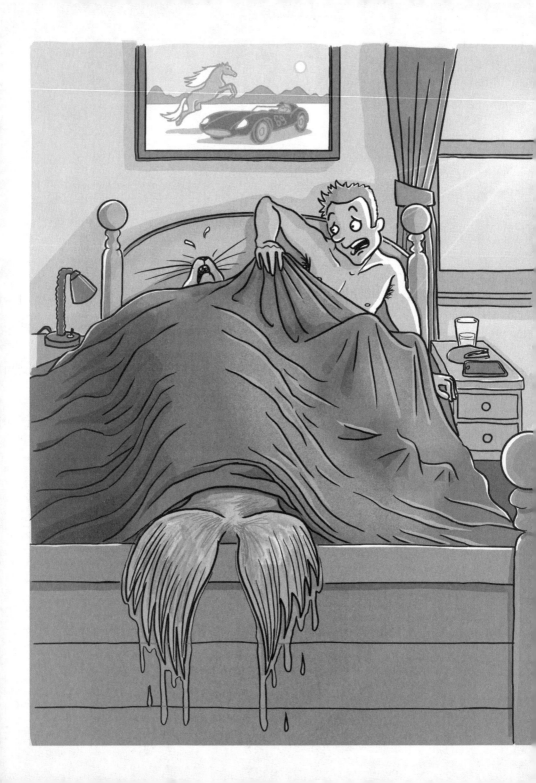

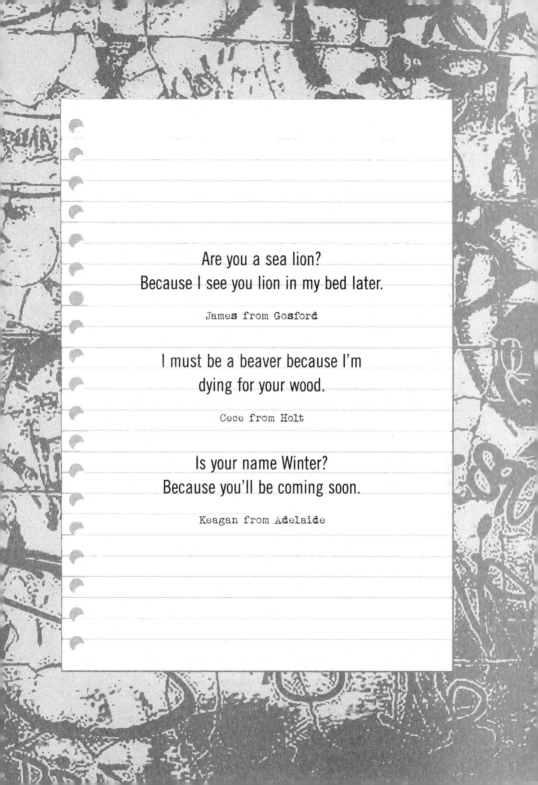

Are you a sea lion?
Because I see you lion in my bed later.

James from Gosford

I must be a beaver because I'm
dying for your wood.

Cece from Holt

Is your name Winter?
Because you'll be coming soon.

Keagan from Adelaide

Are your legs made of Nutella?
Because I'd love to spread them.

Corey from the Gold Coast

Are you Flappy Bird?
Because I'd love to tap you all day long.

Lachlan from Pakenham

Is that a ladder on your pants?
Or a stairway to heaven?

Dean from Hornsby

Are those pants from space?
Because that ass is out of this world.

Sylvia from Fremantle

My love for you is just like diarrhea,
I just can't hold it in.

Leslie from Rockhampton

Damn girl, your bone structure . . .
is giving my bone structure.

Randy from Mollymook

Are you a drill sergeant?
Because you have my privates
standing at attention.

Eric from Green Valley

My dream is to be an astronaut . . .
So I can explore Uranus.

Justin from Caringbah South

There are lots of things we don't know
about the universe . . .
All I know is that it starts with u n i.

Allan from West Albury

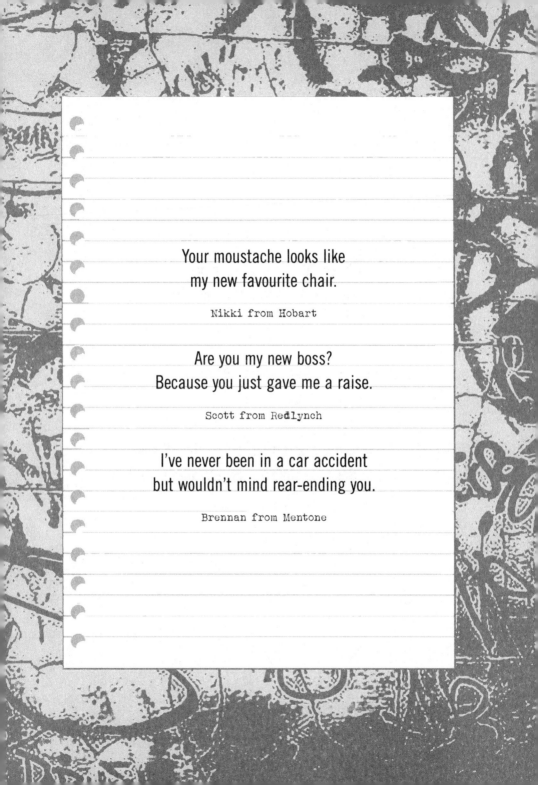

Your moustache looks like
my new favourite chair.

Nikki from Hobart

Are you my new boss?
Because you just gave me a raise.

Scott from Redlynch

I've never been in a car accident
but wouldn't mind rear-ending you.

Brennan from Mentone

I have 206 bones in my body . . .
But when I see you I have 207.

Sal from Canberra

I love Ronaldo, but I think we should get Messi.

Ralph from Brisbane

Damn girl are you sitting on the F5 key?
Because that ass is refreshing.

Kurt from Hobart

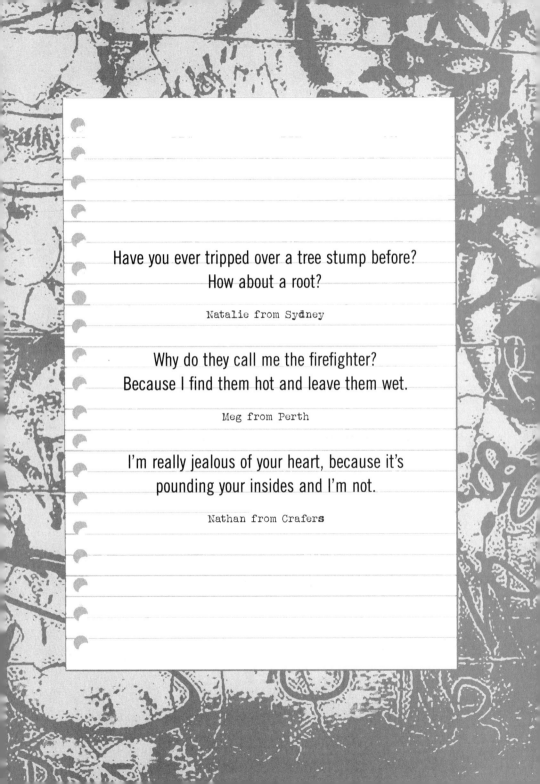

Have you ever tripped over a tree stump before?
How about a root?

Natalie from Sydney

Why do they call me the firefighter?
Because I find them hot and leave them wet.

Meg from Perth

I'm really jealous of your heart, because it's
pounding your insides and I'm not.

Nathan from Crafers

Do you like chocolate because I've got half a bar.

Joseph from Newcastle

You make me wanna dive into that sea.
That pus-sea.

Steven from Hurstville

Can you change your name to Awesome for me?
Because I want to tell everyone
I'm fucking Awesome.

Eric from Launceston

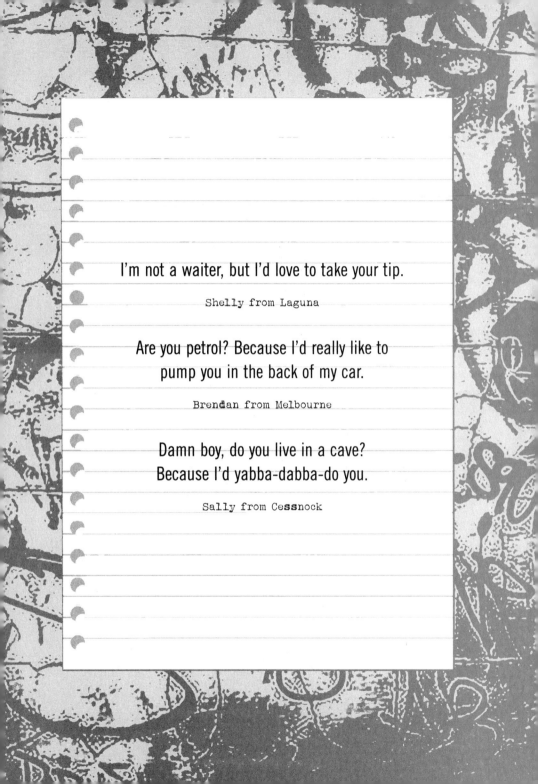

I'm not a waiter, but I'd love to take your tip.

Shelly from Laguna

Are you petrol? Because I'd really like to
pump you in the back of my car.

Brendan from Melbourne

Damn boy, do you live in a cave?
Because I'd yabba-dabba-do you.

Sally from Cessnock

Are you a rollercoaster?
Because I would ride you.

Renae from the Gold Coast

My mum raised a gentleman but you,
you raise my penis.

David from Melbourne

I may not be the Hulk but I'm ready to smash.

Jason from Penrith

If I flip a coin, what do you reckon
my chances are of getting head?

Harry from Dubbo

I wanna paint you green and spank you
like a disobedient avocado.

Natalie from Adelaide

Is your name osteoporosis?
Because you are giving me a serious
bone condition.

Reece from Canberra

My sheets are black.
Want to make them white?

Jess from Sydney

Have you got any Italian in you?
Do you want some?

Abbie from Melbourne

Do you want to go turkey shooting?
I'll shoot and you gobble.

Toby from Brisbane

Want to play lion tamer?
You get on all fours and
I'll put my head in your mouth.

James from Launceston

I left my blow job at your house.
Can I come over and get it?

Rog from Fremantle

Are you a doctor?
Because you just cured my erectile dysfunction.

Keegan from Lane Cove

PICK-UP LINES YOU COULD* USE

*Jimmy & Nath Disclaimer: Results may vary dramatically—use these lines at your own risk!

You know what you would look really beautiful in?
My arms.

Blake from Revesby

I believe in following my dreams . . .
can I have your Instagram?

Belle from Sydney

Are you a charger?
Because I'm dying without you.

Sabrina from Eastlands

If you were a transformer, you'd be Optimus Fine.

Dave from Kingston

Are you a bank loan?
Because you have my interest.

Archer from Brisbane

Is your name Chamomile?
Because you are a hot-tea.

Emma from Paddington

Your eyes are like Ikea.
I could get lost in them for hours.

Rachel from Arncliffe

Are you sunburnt? Or are you always this hot?

Ellen from Peakhurst

Let's flip a coin. Tails I'm yours, heads you're mine.

Luke from Broadmeadow

If you were words on a page, you'd be fine print.

Bec from Newcastle

I think there's something wrong with my phone . . .
could you call it and see if it works?

Jason from Miranda

Is your name Google?
Because you are everything
I have been searching for.

Taylor from Leichhardt

I'm writing an article on the finer things in life . . .
I was hoping I could interview you.

Cathy from Lilli Pilli

Are you a Minecraft fence?
Because I can't get over you.

Chloe from Sandy Bay

Did you just come out of the oven?
Because you are hot.

Edward from Perth

Some people won't admit to their faults . . .
I would, if I had any.

Cherie from Perth

Is it hot in here? Or is it just you?

Jack from Dulwich Hill

You must be a yoghurt because
I want to spoon you.

Evie from Perth

The barista may forget your name . . .
but I never will.

Serena from Townsville

I'm not bragging or anything but when I get naked
. . . the shower gets turned on.

Rachel from Berry

I'd like to take you to the movies . . .
but they don't let you bring your own snacks.

Jake from Hawthorne

Are you a keyboard?
Because you are just my type.

Michael from Inala

Are you a time traveller?
Because I see you in my future.

Robert from Redhill

I'm not currently an organ donor . . .
but I'd love to give you my heart.

Ethan from Holland Park

Your hand seems pretty heavy . . .
let me hold it for you.

Holly from Forest Hill

Are you rocky road?
Because I'm nuts for you.

Bianca from Heathcote

Hey, there's a sale in my room,
clothes are 100 per cent off.

Noel from Robertson

Are you from the Netherlands?
Because Amsterdammmmn.

Josh from Bulwer

Do you have a bandaid by any chance?
Because I hurt my knee falling for you.

Jarram from West Footscray

Are you from Tennessee?
Because you're the only ten I see.

Jasmine from Coffs Harbour

Are you from KFC?
Because you are finger-licking good.

Emma from Adelaide

Are you an ibis?
Cos I've bin-chicken you out.

Luke from Hobart

Hey girl are you a microwave?
Because mmmmmmmm.

Rich from Melbourne

Do you like raisins?
How do you feel about a date?

Reg from Port Melbourne

Are you wi-fi?
Because I have a strong fast
connection to you.

Mary from Castle Hill

Are you a parking ticket?
Because you've got fine written all over you.

Evan from Kangaroo Point

Of all your curves, your smile is my favourite.

Olivia from Karuah

I'm gonna sue Spotify because they did not list you
as the hottest single of the week.

Ashley from The Entrance

Forget about Spider-Man, Superman and Batman;
I'll be your man.

Adrian from Preston

Are you a scientist?
Because I want to do you on the table periodically.

Claire from the Sunshine Coast

Do you know CPR?
Because you have taken my breath away.

Brendan from Melbourne

Are you a Sharpie? Because you're ultra fine.

Lisa from Gymea Bay

MED -ICAL MIS- HAPS

Accidents, health issues and medical mayhem

Did you hear about the guy who dipped his testicles in glitter? Yeah, pretty nuts.

Deano from Pakenham

What do a dentist and a gynaecologist have in common? They both want to know when your last filling was.

Anthony from Kilmore

I swallowed two pieces of string . . . When they came out the other end they were tied together, I shit you knot.

Brooke from Dickson

My uncle died drinking furniture polish. It was a slow death but a really nice finish.

Nathan from Thrumster

What do accountants do when they're constipated? They work it out with a pencil.

Tom from Lane Cove

What do a near-sighted gynaecologist and a puppy have in common? A wet nose.

Emily from Ingleburn

What do you call an Englishman who has penises for thighs?
Cockney.

Di from Bonner

What's the difference between an oral thermometer and a rectal thermometer?
The taste.

Jackson from Fremantle

Why do people say grow some balls? Balls are weak and sensitive. If you really wanna get tough, grow a vagina! Those can take a pounding.

Katie from Dapto

Who's the highest ranking officer at the hospital?
General Anaesthesia.

Raymond from Penshurst

A man was rushed to the emergency room after inserting ten plastic horses into his rectum . . . Doctors have described his condition as stable.

Anthony from Kilmore

Is it possible to give someone a skin graft from your butt?
Ass skin for a friend.

Kelly from Avalon

I accidentally rubbed ketchup in my eyes, now I have Heinzsight.

Anna from Moorooka

I started a support group for men with erectile dysfunction. It was a total flop and nobody came.

Jacko from Warringah

Which five-letter body part is long and flexible and contains the letters p, e, n, i and s?
Spine.

Esther from Robina

What do you call a person with no
body and no nose?
No body nose.

Noel from Canberra

Did you know that diarrhea is
hereditary? Yeah, it runs in your jeans.

Blake from the Mornington Peninsula

I visited the doctor today and he said
my sugar was too high, so I came home
and moved it to a lower shelf.

Bianca from Heathcote

I accidentally swallowed a load
of Scrabble tiles . . .
My next shit could spell disaster.

Rory from the Gold Coast

I took the cat's medicine this morning
. . . Don't ask meow.

Catherine from Gymea

What did the psychiatrist say to the
man wrapped in plastic?
I can clearly see your nuts.

Blake from Hobart

Why do your heart, liver and
lungs all fit in your body?
Because they are well organ-ised.

Arnold from Kirrawee

What did one vagina lip say to the other? We used to be so tight.

Emily from Ingleburn

What do you call a redhead with a yeast infection? Gingerbread.

Brooke from Erskineville

What's the difference between a vampire and a person suffering from anaemia?
One sucks blood and the other's blood sucks.

Mon from Adelaide

Why was the man unhappy with his discount circumcision?
Because it was a bloody rip-off.

Ed from Brisbane

What do you call a urologist on social media?
A TikTok dick doc.

Pete from Coalcliff

FAMILY AND RELATIONSHIPS

Mums, dads, marriages and mistakes

Why didn't the skeleton go to the ball?
Because he had no body to go with.

Emily from Ingleburn

What's a group of chubby newborns
called?
Heavy infantry.

Daniel from Mount Lawley

My girlfriend is a body builder . . .
She's pregnant.

Oliver from North Adelaide

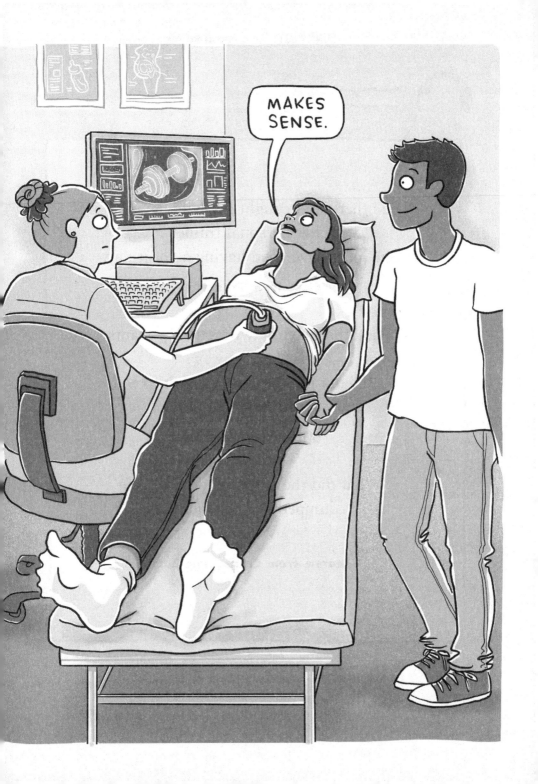

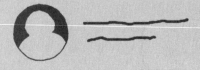

The other day I caught my wife having sex
with her personal trainer . . .
She must have been having a cheat day.

Blake from Frankston

The other day my wife said she wants
another baby . . .
Thank god because I didn't like
the first one either.

Blake from Frankston

What did the cannibal do after she
dumped her boyfriend?
Wiped.

Leanne from Cranbourne East

I had to break up with my girlfriend, because she couldn't stop counting . . .
I wonder what she is up to now.

Steve from Canberra

How do you get a farm girl to marry you?
First, a tractor.

Carlo from Broome

My girlfriend said we could have three hall passes each. She picked Henry Cavill, Jason Momoa and Matt Damon. Apparently her sister, our kid's teacher and Kelsey in the marketing department were the wrong answers.

Anthony from Kilmore

I was named after my dad
because I couldn't possibly have been
named before him.

Ash from Launceston

Do you know the saying one man's trash is
another man's treasure?
Wonderful saying, horrible way to find out
you are adopted.

Jordan from Wollongong

What's the down side of being
a test-tube baby?
You know your dad is a wanker.

Ray from Charlestown

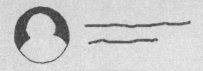

My girlfriend is furious at our neighbour who sunbathes naked in her backyard. Personally, I'm on the fence.

James from Kelvin Grove

My girlfriend changed after she became a vegetarian. It's like I've never seen herbivore.

Stas from Yatala

Why do some couples go to the gym? Because they want their relationship to work out.

Brad from Maitland

My girlfriend borrowed $100 from me. After three years, when we separated, she returned exactly $100. I lost interest in that relationship.

Luna from Tugun

My girlfriend dumped me because I didn't ejaculate very far . . .
It's one of my shortcomings.

Blake from Frankston

The other day my girlfriend asked me why
I never buy her flowers.
I said, 'I didn't realise you sold them.'

Vanessa from Newcastle

I once had a girlfriend who was cross-
eyed. But we had to break up, because she
was seeing someone on the side.

Nicole from Parramatta

TECH NO LOL OGY

Science, gadgets and modern innovations

What does a robot do after sex?
Nuts and bolts.

Rose from Canberra

My friend quit his job at BMW. He of course gave no indication he was leaving.

Liam from Battery Point

My Bluetooth speaker wasn't working so I threw it in the ocean . . .
Now it's syncing.

Ava from Braddon

What is the friendliest element in the periodic table?
Hi-drogen.

Henry from Rockhampton

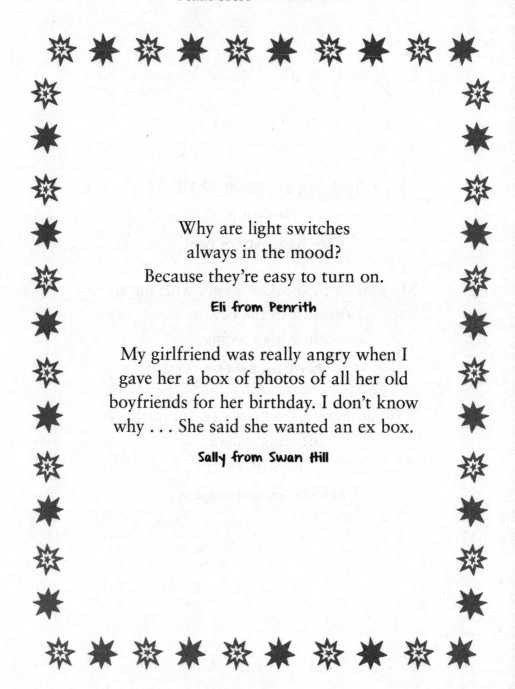

Why are light switches
always in the mood?
Because they're easy to turn on.

Eli from Penrith

My girlfriend was really angry when I
gave her a box of photos of all her old
boyfriends for her birthday. I don't know
why . . . She said she wanted an ex box.

Sally from Swan Hill

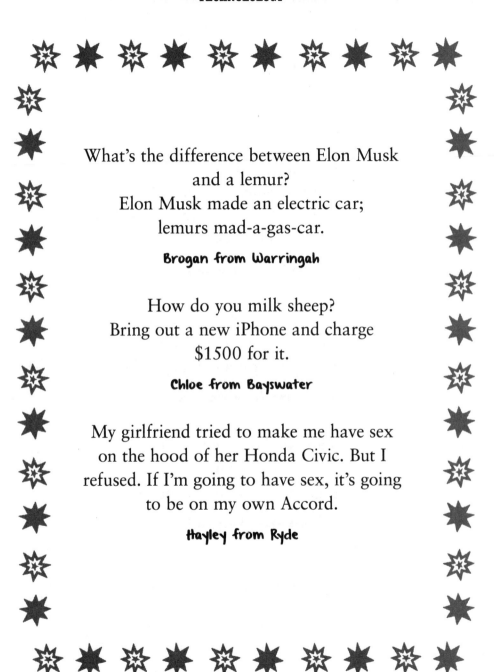

What's the difference between Elon Musk
and a lemur?
Elon Musk made an electric car;
lemurs mad-a-gas-car.

Brogan from Warringah

How do you milk sheep?
Bring out a new iPhone and charge
$1500 for it.

Chloe from Bayswater

My girlfriend tried to make me have sex
on the hood of her Honda Civic. But I
refused. If I'm going to have sex, it's going
to be on my own Accord.

Hayley from Ryde

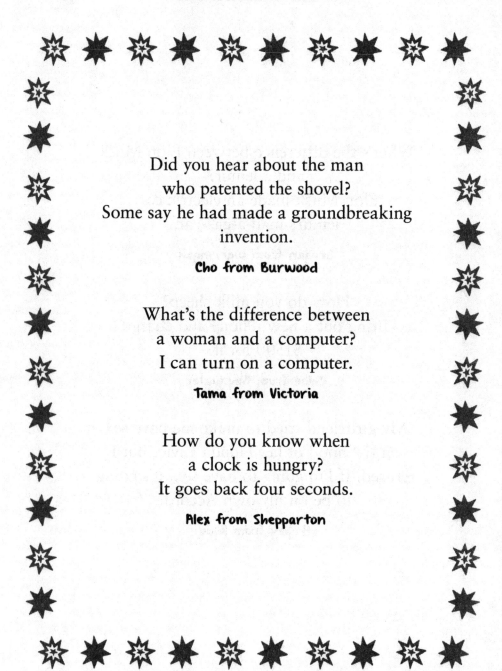

Did you hear about the man
who patented the shovel?
Some say he had made a groundbreaking
invention.

Cho from Burwood

What's the difference between
a woman and a computer?
I can turn on a computer.

Tama from Victoria

How do you know when
a clock is hungry?
It goes back four seconds.

Alex from Shepparton

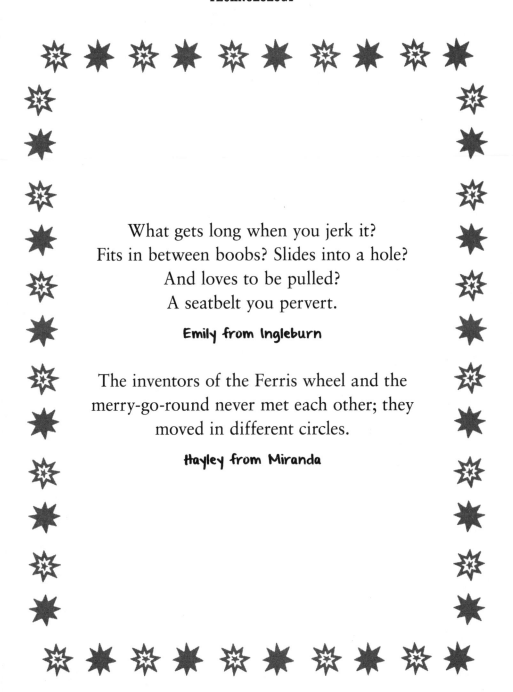

What gets long when you jerk it?
Fits in between boobs? Slides into a hole?
And loves to be pulled?
A seatbelt you pervert.

Emily from Ingleburn

The inventors of the Ferris wheel and the
merry-go-round never met each other; they
moved in different circles.

Hayley from Miranda

FOOD AND COOKING

A buffet of lols

What do you get when you cross a dick
with a potato?
A dictator.

Henry from Brisbane

What's the difference between
hungry and horny?
Where you put the cucumber.

Robin from Tieri

How does German bread say hello?
Gluten-tag.

Ash from Dandenong

The guy that invented sprinkles died . . .
Hundreds and thousands came to his
funeral.

Anthony from Kilmore

What do you call a pea
that rolls off your plate?
An escapea.

Charlotte from Deakin

I got hit in the head with a can of soda
recently . . . Luckily it was a soft drink.

Edward from Kingsford

What did the full glass say to the empty
glass? Go home, you look drunk.

Adrian from Yarra Bend

What do you call it when a hen looks
at lettuce?
Chicken sees a salad.

Ashley from Muswellbrook

Did you hear about the guy
who tried to eat a train?
He bit off more than he could choo-choo.

Caitlyn from Maroubra

Walking home last night I passed a slice of
apple pie, a hot fudge sundae and a lemon
cheesecake. I thought to myself . . .
the streets are strangely desserted.

Ariane from South Morang

What do you get when you cross an armed robbery with a chicken schnitzel?
Schnitty schnitty bang bang.

John from Surfers Paradise

What did the grape say when it was crushed?
Nothing, it just let out a little wine.

Casey from Campbelltown

Why did the coffee call the police?
It got mugged.

Erica from Parramatta

Why was the mushroom invited to the party?
Because he is a fungi.

Kim from Berkeley Vale

What smells better than it tastes?
A nose.

Justin from Hurstville

Why did the baked beans move to Queensland?
Because they wanted to be in Cairns.

Ryan from Melbourne

I've been telling people about the benefits
of eating dried grapes . . .
You know, raisin awareness.

Carrie from Seven Hills

What do you call a food fight with an
unlimited amount of food?
All you can yeet.

Carmen from Hoxton Park

What's the difference between
an egg and a beetroot?
You can beat an egg but you
can't beet a root.

Brayden from Geelong

Did you hear about the cannibal who was
late for dinner?
He was given the cold shoulder.

Inara from Currumbin

My son asked me why I was knocking on
the fridge. I said there might be
a salad dressing.

John from Canberra

Which nut is the angriest?
Pissed-achio.

Yevonne from Whittlesea

What's a forklift? Food usually . . .

Eve from Moonee Valley

What is an egg's favourite city?
New Yolk City.

Ash from Dubbo

How does the butcher introduce his wife?
Meet Patty.

Rebecca from Newport

I dropped a bag of flour at the grocery
store . . . I went to pick it up but the
assistant said it was self-raising.

Oscar from Darwin

What cheese is made backwards?
Edam.

Josh from Canberra

Why does Dr Pepper come in a can?
Because his wife died.

Tom from Melbourne

Why does my girlfriend call my penis
Subway?
Because it's six inches long
and smells like a foot.

Anthony from Kilmore

What is hairy on the outside and
wet on the inside, begins with
a c and ends with a t?
A coconut.

Simon from Sydney

What do runners eat?
Fast food.

Caden from Milton

LOLGBT QIA+*

The pride hub

*JIMMY & NATH DISCLAIMER:
These jokes about the LGBTQIA+
community were collected by Jimmy & Nath's
amazing producer Jaryd (who's gay, so these
are okay haha)—he approved them all.

What is a lesbian's favourite Pokémon?
Squirtle.

Shauna from Earlwood

What do you call a lesbian dinosaur?
A lick-a-lot-a-puss.

Robin from Tieri

Did you hear about the bisexual
donkey? He had a he in the morning
and a haw in the afternoon.

Kate from Subiaco

Two deer walk out of a gay bar. One turns to the other and says I can't believe I blew 50 bucks in there.

Tommo from Tumbi Umbi

In a lesbian relationship,
who cooks dinner?
Neither, they both eat out.

Alice from Victoria

My lesbian neighbours recently gave me a Rolex for Christmas . . .
I think they misunderstood when I said, 'I wanna watch.'

Anthony from Kilmore

What did one gay sperm say
to the other gay sperm?
We're never gonna find
an egg in all this shit.

Anthony from Kilmore

What do you call a lesbian
with fat fingers?
Well hung.

Anthony from Kilmore

What do turtles and lesbians have
in common?
They both choke on plastic.

Emily from Ingleburn

What do you call a gay dinosaur?
A megasoreass.

Robin from Tieri

What's a lesbian soccer player's
favourite strike?
The scissor kick.

Shauna from Earlwood

What do you call a gay couple
from Alabama?
Super Smash Bros.

Ayla from Sydney

Why are all the stools in
a gay bar upside down?
So they can seat four.

Sarah from Darwin

USEFUL WORKPLACE NICKNAMES

Noodles—thinks all jobs take two minutes.

Jacob from Lilyfield

Haemorrhoid—pain in the ass.

Scott from Melbourne

Slinky—good for nothing but fun to push down the stairs.

Claire from Bankstown

Shania—they don't impress you much.

Taylor from Padstow

Bushranger—always holding everyone up.

Kurt from Miranda

G-spot—because you can never find him.

Karen from Heathmont

Mastercard—because they take credit for everything.

Amanda from Adelaide

The Blister—only shows up once the
hard work is done.

David from Sydney

Glovebox—because every time he opened his
mouth, crap fell out.

Fiona from Milperra

Lantern—not very bright and has to be carried.

Jeremy from Kangaroo Point

Foreskin—when things got hard he would disappear.

Jess from Tenambit

Paper Straw—someone who works but not for long.

Peter from Sydney

Golf Ball—someone who is hard to find.

Garry from Tempe

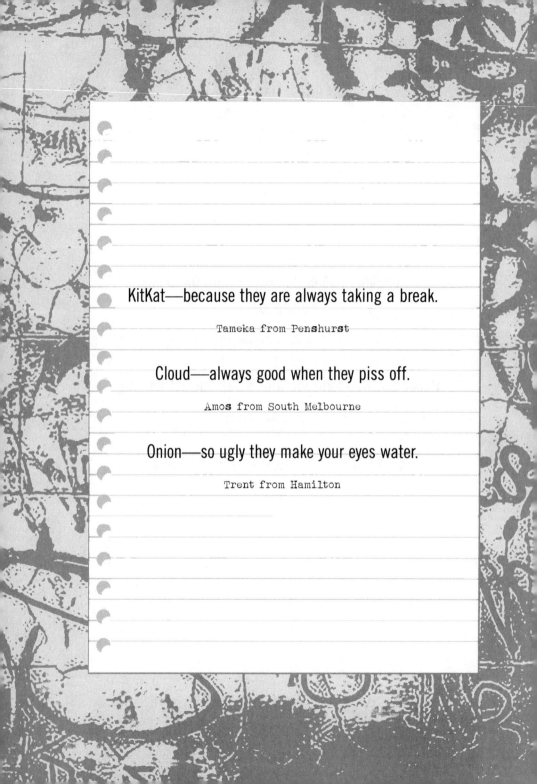

KitKat—because they are always taking a break.

Tameka from Penshurst

Cloud—always good when they piss off.

Amos from South Melbourne

Onion—so ugly they make your eyes water.

Trent from Hamilton

Hostage—always tied up with something.

Kade from Canberra

Poo Fingers—because everything they touch turns to shit.

Douglas from Hobart

Birthday Cake—because everyone got a piece.

Angel from South Melbourne

Drill Bit—because they are a small boring tool.

Mike from Auburn

Optus—because five minutes on the phone with them ruins your entire day.

Natalie from Belmore

Singlet—because they are always on your back.

Tyler from Melbourne

Liz Hayes—because they only work for 60 minutes.

Natalie from Sydney

Two Dicks—because they are too much of a
wanker for just one dick.

Rob from Sydney

Contagious—took the cunt ages to do anything.

Josh from Melbourne

Panadol—because they give you a headache
whenever they're around.

Rikki from Perth

Morphine—slow-acting dope.

Ailish from Hobart

Lightning—because they are so shit with a
hammer, they never hit the same place twice.

Nathan from Sydney

The Midwife—they always deliver but they spend
most of the day surrounded by cunts.

Jenny from Sydney

POP CULT CHA HA HA

Famous characters, books, movies and TV shows

What do the Starship Enterprise and a piece of toilet paper have in common? They both circle Uranus in search for Cling-ons.

Sarah from South Melbourne

→ **Speaking of poo** . . . *Jimmy was once at Melbourne Airport with a bad case of food poisoning. All the stalls in the men's bathroom were taken, so he ran out and found a disabled toilet. There was no one waiting, and he was getting desperate. He sat down and did what he needed to do. But as he started wiping he could hear some children crying . . . the automatic doors for the disabled toilet had opened and there was a small line of children in wheelchairs staring at him as he wiped his bum. He pulled his pants up and ran, apologising, only to see them all again later as he boarded the plane . . .*

Singing in the shower is fun until you get
soap in your mouth, then it's a soap opera.

Rosie from Moonah

What does a Pokémon say when they've
had too much sex?
Vulva sore.

Hannah from Henley Beach

I was reading a great book about an
immortal dog the other day . . .
It was impossible to put down.

Lily from Nightcliff

How much does Santa pay to park his sleigh?
Nothing, it's on the house.

Anthony from Kilmore

What do you call a wizard who falls down the stairs?
Tumbledore.

Ray from the Sunshine Coast

How does Darth Vader like his toast?
On the dark side.

Nicole from Quakers Hill

What do you call
James Bond taking a bath?
Bubble 07.

Carla from Ultimo

What do you call a constipated detective?
No Shit Sherlock.

Ephram from Silverwater

⟶ **Nath has a** *constipation story to add here. He was once on holiday with his partner in Hawaii and woke up in the middle of the night writhing in pain. It was so bad that he couldn't walk, and he thought his appendix must have burst, so his partner called an ambulance to take him to emergency surgery. By the time the ambulance arrived he was practically screaming, but then suddenly he felt like he needed to go to the toilet. Turns out there was nothing wrong with his appendix at all, and all the pain was relieved once a shit the size of Waikiki hit the water. The ambulance fee still had to be paid, unfortunately.*

Why is Medusa the hottest character in
Greek mythology?
Because every time you look at her
you get rock hard.

Jerry from Canberra

Why don't witches have children?
Because warlocks have hollow weenies and
crystal balls.

Steff from Kooringal

I think I got scammed while watching
Pennywise porn . . .
I never saw 'It' coming.

Benjamin from Glenelg

What do you call a superhero with no
sense of direction?
Wander Woman.

Claire from Rosny

Who is the roundest knight at King
Arthur's table?
Circumference.

Anthony from Kilmore

What happened after Snow White sat in
the bath feeling happy?
Happy got out, so she felt Grumpy.

Greg from Manly

⟶ **Nath once heard** *an ad on the radio
(of all places) calling out for 'the next Disney
superstar who would be taken to LA', so
he drove two hours, got a haircut and put
on a nice shirt to join 400 children aged
between five and ten in a big auditorium
in the middle of nowhere. Important side
note: he was 20 years old. He was asked
to deliver one pre-prepared line to show
off his acting skills. The line was something
like, 'My tooth is sore, it's time to go to*

the dentist.' After he delivered it, the talent scout slow-clapped then announced, 'This man is going to be a star!' Nath was so excited. As he left he was given a letter to take home which explained how 'being a star' would work. All he now had to do was pay a small fee of US$50,000 to get over to LA where there was an actors' conference and he might *be picked up as an extra on the TV show* Wizards of Waverly Place . . . *It's safe to say that this is where Nath's Disney career ended.*

What's Peter Pan's favourite place to
eat out?
Wendy's.

David from Miranda

Why does a mermaid wear seashells?
She outgrew her B-shells.

Jessica from Adelaide

Did you hear Mickey Mouse is divorcing
Minnie because she did something silly?
Yeah she was fucking Goofy.

Sophie from Wagga Wagga

What did Mario say when he broke up
with Princess Peach?
It's not you, it's a me, Mario.

Chloe from Woolooware

How did Pinocchio find out he was made
of wood?
His hand caught on fire.

Simon from Sydney

CELEB-RITY SILL-IES

The rich and the famous

→ **Speaking of celebrities** . . . *Jimmy was once at a Sydney Swans game (that's Australian Rules Football) in Sydney, and ran into Sydney Sweeney, who was in Australia filming* Anyone But You. *He started flirting with her and got a photo . . . and then ruined it by saying, 'You know what's funny? Your name is Sydney and you're in Sydney! Hahahaha!' He never saw her again . . .*

What do you call Christina Aguilera, Justin Timberlake and Jessica Simpson? Britney's peers.

John from Moonee Ponds

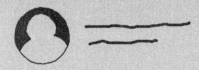

What singer pees a lot?
Urethra Franklin.

Isaac from Sydney

Someone asked me if I liked Gwen Stefani
. . . I said no doubt.

Edward from Randwick

Why didn't Michael Jackson drink coffee?
Because he preferred tea-hee.

Ella from Belmont

Which pop star do penguins hate?
Seal.

Kiera from Footscray

→ **Fun fact:** *We once saw Seal struggling to eat hot chips by himself on a wharf. He had eaten one that was clearly way too hot and started panting and panicking as the chip burnt his tongue. It's good to know that even famous people can't wait to eat their hot chippies.*

Why is Dwayne Johnson the only man who can turn lesbians?
Because Rock beats scissors.

Leanne from Cranbourne East

→ **Fun fact:** *The actual Dwayne the Rock Johnson saw and shared this joke on Instagram and TikTok to over 700 million people and we fucking lost our minds.*

How does the Rock pee?
He Dwaynes his Johnson.

Leanne from Cranbourne East

I lost Dwayne Johnson's cutting tool for the origami workshop . . . Can't believe I lost the Rock's paper scissors.

Allan from Rockhampton

What is it called when Einstein masturbates?
A stroke of genius.

Deano from Pakenham

Why don't vampires attack Taylor Swift?
She's got bad blood.

Winona from Fortitude Valley

How do you find Will Smith in the snow?
You follow the Fresh Prints.

Dannielle from Victoria

I didn't know that Sylvester Stallone
was on his third marriage . . .
I guess his first one was rocky, and his
second one was rocky too.

Ewan from Caringbah

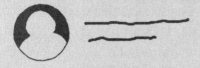

What did 50 Cent do when he was hungry?
58.

Eric from Liverpool

What did 50 Cent say when he was given a sweater by his grandma?
G-u-nit.

Leanne from Cranbourne East

→ **Fun fact:** *Leanne, who is a regular on our show, delivered this joke live to 50 Cent when we interviewed him. We were asked not to film the interview, however we did anyway and posted the video, and 50 Cent also loved it so much he shared it on his Instagram.*

I asked my mum for money to go to a 50 Cent concert. She said sure, here's $1 so you can take your sister too.

Steph from Melbourne

What do you get when you play country
music backwards?
You get back your dog, your wife
and your truck.

Justin from Toowoomba

What's an archer's favourite musician
and band?
David Bowe and Arrowsmith.

Brooke from Perth

RANDOM RIDICULOUS-NESS

The silly, the nonsensical and the completely unexpected

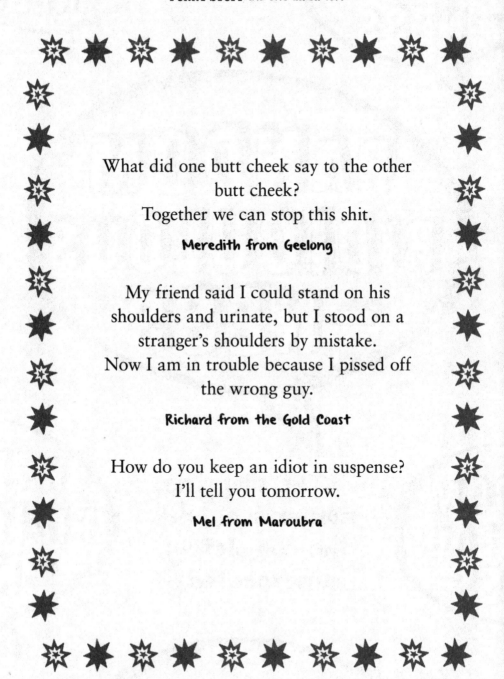

What did one butt cheek say to the other
butt cheek?
Together we can stop this shit.

Meredith from Geelong

My friend said I could stand on his
shoulders and urinate, but I stood on a
stranger's shoulders by mistake.
Now I am in trouble because I pissed off
the wrong guy.

Richard from the Gold Coast

How do you keep an idiot in suspense?
I'll tell you tomorrow.

Mel from Maroubra

What do you call an old snowman?
A glass of water.

Craig from Cygnet

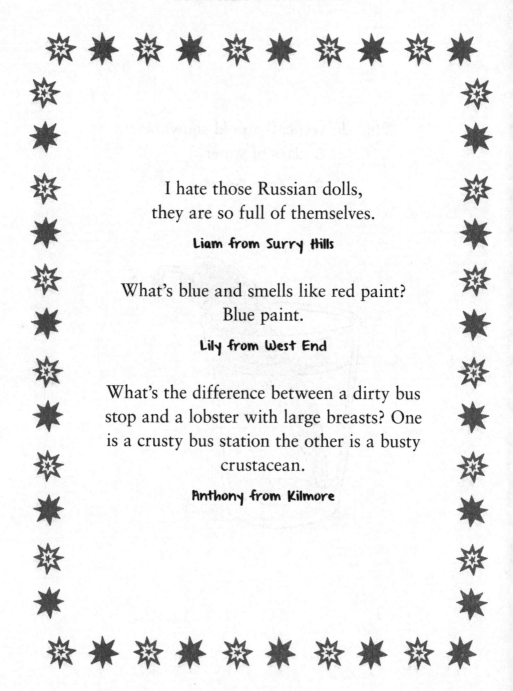

I hate those Russian dolls,
they are so full of themselves.

Liam from Surry Hills

What's blue and smells like red paint?
Blue paint.

Lily from West End

What's the difference between a dirty bus
stop and a lobster with large breasts? One
is a crusty bus station the other is a busty
crustacean.

Anthony from Kilmore

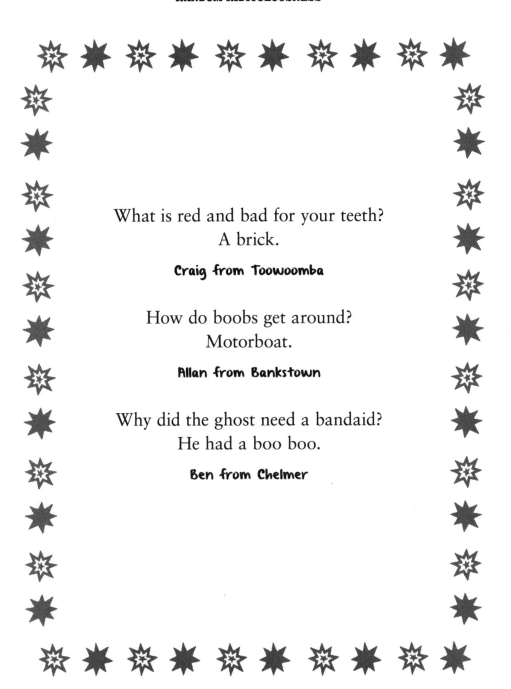

What is red and bad for your teeth?
A brick.

Craig from Toowoomba

How do boobs get around?
Motorboat.

Allan from Bankstown

Why did the ghost need a bandaid?
He had a boo boo.

Ben from Chelmer

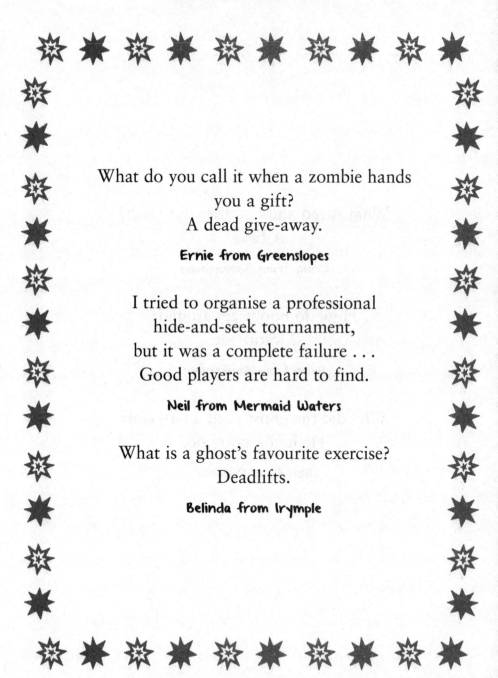

What do you call it when a zombie hands
you a gift?
A dead give-away.

Ernie from Greenslopes

I tried to organise a professional
hide-and-seek tournament,
but it was a complete failure . . .
Good players are hard to find.

Neil from Mermaid Waters

What is a ghost's favourite exercise?
Deadlifts.

Belinda from Irymple

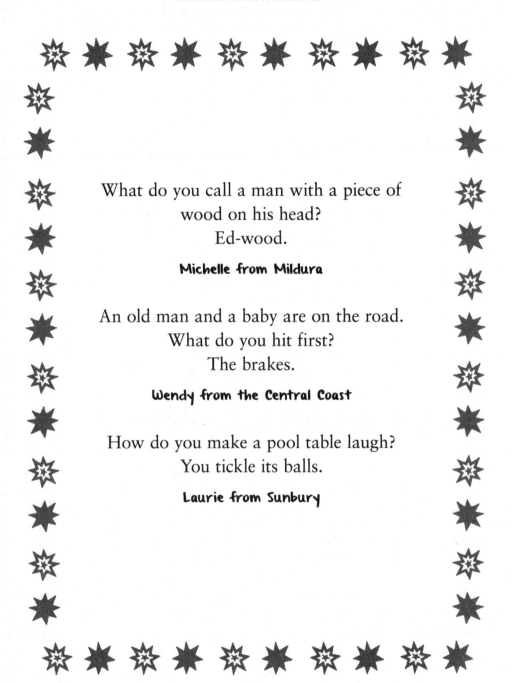

What do you call a man with a piece of
wood on his head?
Ed-wood.

Michelle from Mildura

An old man and a baby are on the road.
What do you hit first?
The brakes.

Wendy from the Central Coast

How do you make a pool table laugh?
You tickle its balls.

Laurie from Sunbury

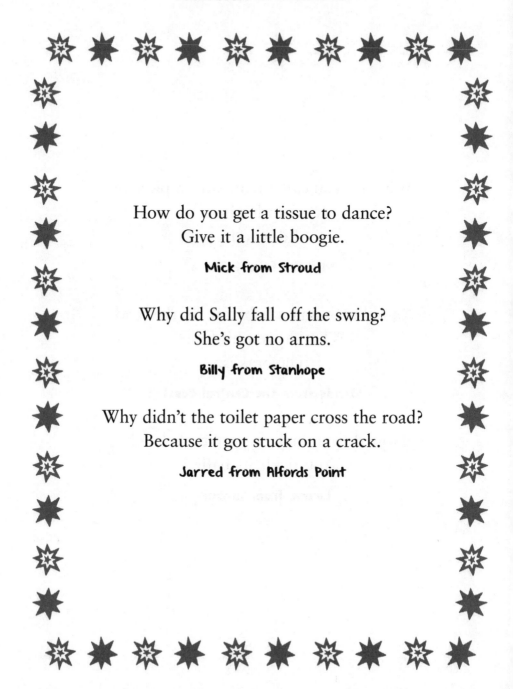

How do you get a tissue to dance?
Give it a little boogie.

Mick from Stroud

Why did Sally fall off the swing?
She's got no arms.

Billy from Stanhope

Why didn't the toilet paper cross the road?
Because it got stuck on a crack.

Jarred from Alfords Point

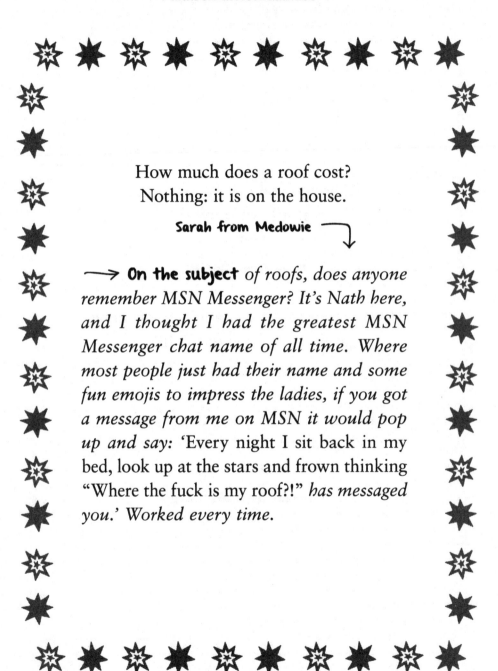

How much does a roof cost?
Nothing: it is on the house.

Sarah from Medowie

⟶ **On the subject** *of roofs, does anyone remember MSN Messenger? It's Nath here, and I thought I had the greatest MSN Messenger chat name of all time. Where most people just had their name and some fun emojis to impress the ladies, if you got a message from me on MSN it would pop up and say:* 'Every night I sit back in my bed, look up at the stars and frown thinking "Where the fuck is my roof?!" *has messaged you.' Worked every time.*

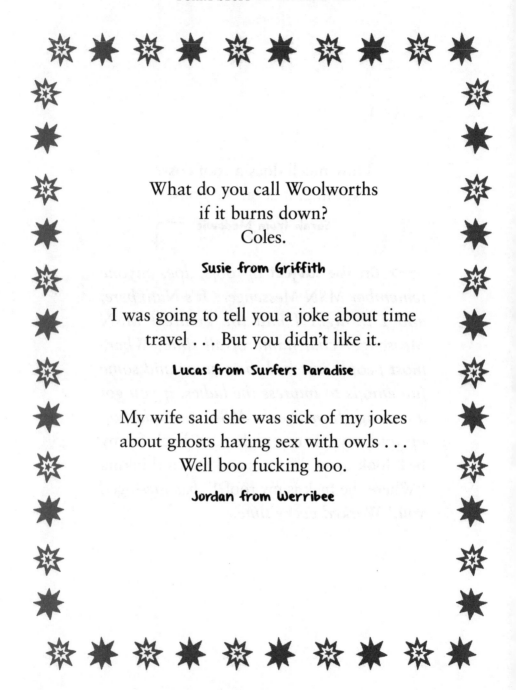

What do you call Woolworths
if it burns down?
Coles.

Susie from Griffith

I was going to tell you a joke about time
travel . . . But you didn't like it.

Lucas from Surfers Paradise

My wife said she was sick of my jokes
about ghosts having sex with owls . . .
Well boo fucking hoo.

Jordan from Werribee

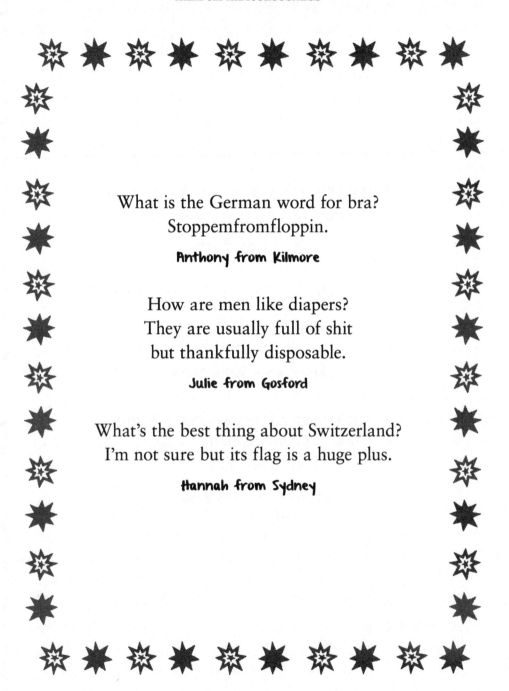

What is the German word for bra?
Stoppemfromfloppin.

Anthony from Kilmore

How are men like diapers?
They are usually full of shit
but thankfully disposable.

Julie from Gosford

What's the best thing about Switzerland?
I'm not sure but its flag is a huge plus.

Hannah from Sydney

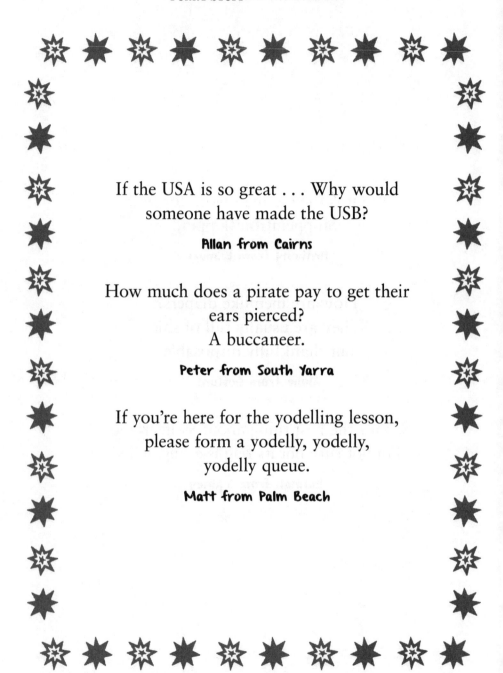

If the USA is so great . . . Why would
someone have made the USB?

Allan from Cairns

How much does a pirate pay to get their
ears pierced?
A buccaneer.

Peter from South Yarra

If you're here for the yodelling lesson,
please form a yodelly, yodelly,
yodelly queue.

Matt from Palm Beach

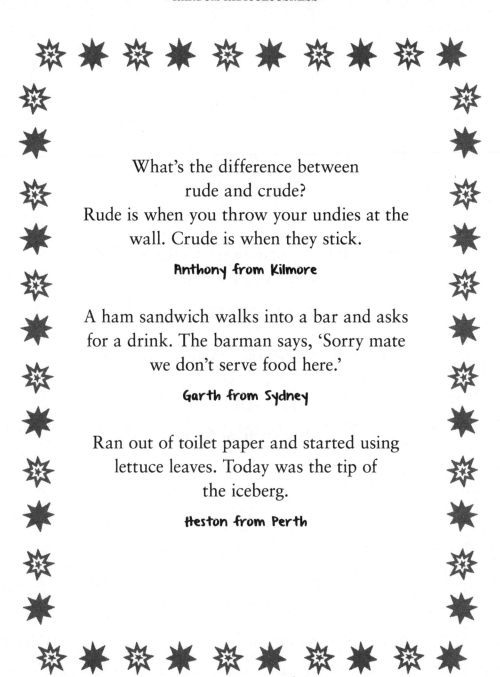

What's the difference between
rude and crude?
Rude is when you throw your undies at the
wall. Crude is when they stick.

Anthony from Kilmore

A ham sandwich walks into a bar and asks
for a drink. The barman says, 'Sorry mate
we don't serve food here.'

Garth from Sydney

Ran out of toilet paper and started using
lettuce leaves. Today was the tip of
the iceberg.

Heston from Perth

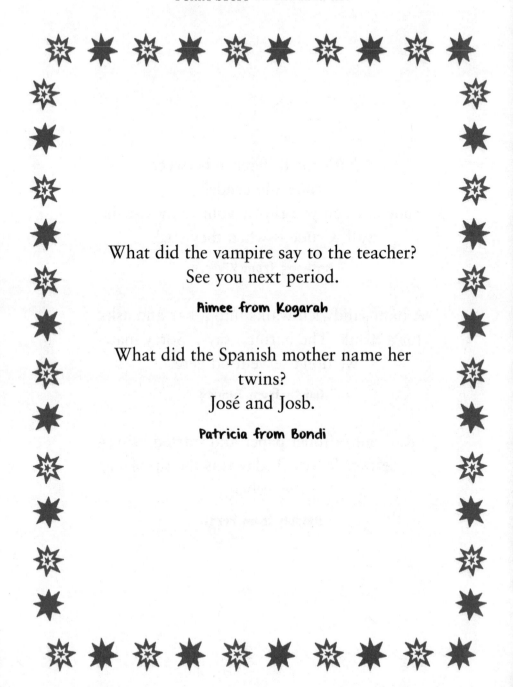

What did the vampire say to the teacher?
See you next period.

Aimee from Kogarah

What did the Spanish mother name her twins?
José and Josb.

Patricia from Bondi

THE SEALED SECTION

DO NOT OPEN AROUND OTHER PEOPLE WHO CAN READ*

*JIMMY & NATH
DISCLAIMER:
Just so you all know, and you
can't say we didn't warn you, the
following section contains
REAL DIRTY, COOKED JOKES.
If you continue to read, we want
you to know you are now just
as bad as us. No one will judge
you if you skip this chapter.

THE SEALED SECTION

DO NOT OPEN
...OTHER
PEOPLE WHO
CAN READ...

NO, YOU WANT TO KEEP GOING?
THIS IS YOUR LAST CHANCE . . .
OKAY, HAVE FUN YOU SICKO,
SEE YOU ON THE OTHER SIDE.

Two tampons were walking down
the street. Which one said hello first?
Neither, they were both stuck up cunts.

Ronin from Tieri

What's the best thing about your husband
eating you out?
Ten minutes of peace and quiet.

Emily from Ingleburn

My girlfriend called me a sex machine.
Well, her exact words were 'you're a
fucking tool'. But I knew what she meant.

Ethan from Wembley

Why is Vaseline useful during sex?
When you smear it all over the door knob
it stops the kids from coming in.

Leanne from Cranbourne East

What's better than roses on a piano?
Tu-lips on your organ.

Anthony from Kilmore

What's the difference between
flowers and anal?
Flowers make your day, anal makes your
hole weak.

Sash from Ashfield

What did the egg say to the boiling water?
I just got laid and you expect me to be
hard again in three minutes?

Anthony from Kilmore

If your uncle Jack fell off a horse, would
you help your uncle Jack off a horse?

Daniel from Melbourne

Why is Santa's sack so big?
He only comes once a year.

Jacob from Griffith

What do you call the useless
piece of skin on a dick?
The man.

Penny from Taren Point

I used to bang a set of twins. People always asked how I told them apart. It was easy—Jenny always painted her nails purple and Tom had a cock.

Billy from Stanhope

What's worse than two girls running with scissors?
Two girls scissoring with the runs.

Billy from Stanhope

What do you get when you mix human
DNA and goat DNA?
Kicked out of the petting zoo.

Anthony from Kilmore

Why did the semen cross the road?
Because I put the wrong sock on
this morning.

Max from Canberra

What do you find at the end of a rainbow?
My ex, the gold-digging bitch.

Kurt from Hobart

I'm reluctant to tell my girlfriend that I
don't enjoy her sex fetishes, but I really
need to get this shit off my chest.

Anthony from Kilmore

What do tofu and dildos have in common?
They are both meat substitutes.

Candice from Rutherford

Our whole family is really worried about
my grandfather's Viagra addiction . . .
Grandma is taking it particularly hard.

Dave from New Norfolk

Why was the vibrator sent to prison?
Because it was charged with sexual
batteries.

Abbie from Mudgeeraba

What do a burnt pizza, a frozen beer and
a pregnant woman have in common?
In all three cases, some idiot forgot to pull
it out in time.

Max from Melbourne

If your girlfriend starts smoking what
should you do?
Slow down a bit and use a little lubricant.

Mick from Stroud

I finally found my wife's G-spot. Turns out it was in her sister the whole time.

Troy from the Central Coast

Have you ever had sex while camping?
It's fucking in tents.

Liz from Maribyrnong

Why do they name cyclones after women?
Because they are wet and wild when they
come, and they take the house and car
when they leave.

Yolanda from Yeppoon

Why don't females in Alaska wear skirts?
So they don't get chapped lips.

Emily from Ingleburn

What's six inches long, full of semen and
hard as a rock?
The sock under my bed.

Zach from North Lambton

What's the odd one out between a TV, a
washing machine and a woman?
The TV, it's the only one that doesn't leak
when it's fucked.

Sue from Granville

How do you get dick from Richard?
You ask him for it.

Henry from Glen Eira

Did you hear about the man who had his
ashes sprinkled into salsa?
He wanted to tear apart his wife's asshole
one more time.

Chris from Byron Bay

On the weekend I went to a local orgy . . .
Came across so many familiar faces.

Anthony from Kilmore

What is a necrophiliac's favourite band?
Cold Play.

Craig from Albury

What's the difference between a condom
and a coffin?
They both hold something stiff but one's
coming and the other's going.

Shane from Ontario

I started dating this blind girl and she said
I had the biggest cock she's ever felt . . .
I told her she was pulling my leg.

Anthony from Kilmore

What's the difference between a pregnant
woman and a lightbulb?
You can unscrew a lightbulb.

Kirby from Bowral

Why don't vegans moan during sex?
They don't want anyone to know they're
enjoying a piece of meat.

Tracey from Sydney

What is the difference between lust,
love and true love?
It depends on whether you spit,
swallow or gargle.

Leanne from Sydney

I really want the best for my partner,
I want her to suc-ceed in life.
So, I started calling my dick seed.

Cam from Rockhampton

What do you get when you jingle
Santa's balls?
A white Christmas.

Lucinda from Brisbane

Two pensioners were engaging in oral sex.
The old man said, 'I can't stay down here
for too long, it really stinks.'
The old lady said, 'Sorry it's my arthritis.'
Confused, he said, 'Arthritis in your
vagina?'
She replied, 'No, the arthritis is in my
hand, I can't wipe my ass.'

Anthony from Kilmore

JOKES ABOUT ...YA MUM*

You know the drill

*JIMMY & NATH DISCLAIMER:

Just so you all know, we love mums, mums love us, in fact we are both big mummies' boys (shout out to our beautiful mums Sue and Cath) . . . BUT, these are still funny.

What's the difference between your mum
and a mosquito?
Your mum doesn't stop sucking when
I spank her.

Billy from Stanhope

I don't really like your mum jokes because
they are a lot like your mum . . .
Too easy to do.

Eric from Liverpool

What's the difference between
bowls and jugs?
I wasn't playing with your mum's bowls
last night.

Billy from Stanhope

Why is your mum a terrible comedian?
It took her nine months to make a joke.

Wes from Harcourt

What do your mum and a
bartender have in common?
They both give great head.

Mick from Stroud

What's the difference between
a joke and three dicks?
Your mum can't take a joke.

Tony from Cootamundra

What's the difference between
a dollar and a pound?
I don't dollar your mum.

Billy from Stanhope

Why do they call my penis tic tac?
Because it makes your mum's
breath smell so good.

Mick from Stroud

What position produces the ugliest son?
Ask your mother.

Alyssa from Bronte

You are putting on a bit of weight.
That's because every time I fuck your
mum, she gives me a biscuit.

Rappa from Melbourne

What do your family dentist and I have
in common?
We both fill your mum's holes.

Mick from Stroud

Your mum is so ugly, your dad wakes up
every day with morning wouldn't.

Oliver from Bowden

What's the difference between you
and me?
You came *out* your mum.

Mick from Stroud

What's the difference between a condom
and your mother?
A condom wasn't on my dick last night.

Mick from Stroud

Just bought a new washing machine. It
reminds me a bit of your mother. It just
takes a full load so well.

Mick from Stroud

What do you call nuts on the wall?
Walnuts.
What do you call nuts on your chest?
Chestnuts.
What do you call nuts on your chin? My
dick in your mum's mouth.

Mick from Stroud

What's the difference between eating lunch
and having sex?
I don't eat lunch with your mum.

Kurt from Braddon

What's the difference between a freezer
and your mother?
The freezer doesn't fart when I take my
meat out.

Mick from Stroud

MUPP-ET JOKE-S

(Yes, there is a
Muppet jokes section)

What do you get when you have two
green balls in your right hand?
Kermit's undivided attention.

Emily from Ingleburn

What's green, slimy and smells like bacon?
Kermit the Frog's fingers.

Emily from Ingleburn

Why can't Miss Piggy count to 70?
Because at 69 she gets a frog in her throat.

Shauna from Earlwood

What's green and spins around really fast?
Kermit the Frog in a blender.

Emily from Ingleburn

What do Harry Potter and Kermit the Frog's penis have in common?
Hogwarts.

Emily from Ingleburn

→ **Fun fact** *(or more accurately stupid idiot fact) about Nath and involving Harry Potter: Nath is a massive Harry Potter fan, and when he went to Harry Potter World in London, he paid $300 for a wand that he claims 'chose him' (Harry Potter nerds will get that). That wand was lost only weeks later—or perhaps thrown out by Jimmy for being a waste of luggage space. Nath is hoping this book sells well so he can fly back to London and buy another wand, so tell your friends about it.*

INSULTS

Why could the man never be a detective?
Because he couldn't even find the clit.

Leanne from Cranbourne East

I was wondering if you were born on a highway?
I just assumed, because that's where most
accidents happen.

Leanne from Cranbourne East

A little birdy told me that having sex with you is
like cooking food in the microwave at 3 a.m.
The longest minute and a half of my life.

Leanne from Cranbourne East

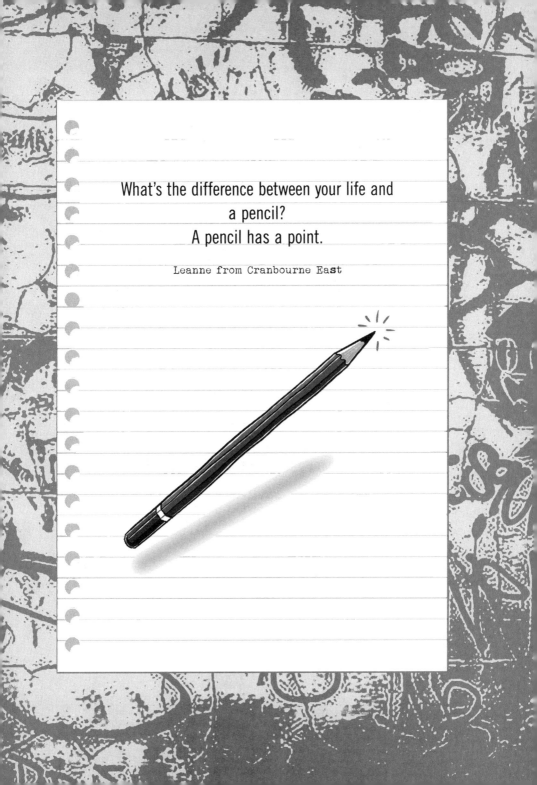

What's the difference between your life and a pencil?
A pencil has a point.

Leanne from Cranbourne East

How many wrinkles does a dickhead have?
Smile, I'll count them for ya.

Emily from Ingleburn

What's the difference between you and a calendar?
A calendar has dates.

Leanne from Cranbourne East

What do you call smart people in the USA?
Tourists.

Sarah from Glendenning

What's the difference between Nath and a brick?
Bricks get laid.

Leanne from Cranbourne East

You are a pizza burn on the roof
of the world's mouth.

Elliot from Brisbane

You are more disappointing than
an unsalted pretzel.

Henry from Preston

If common sense is common,
why are you without it?

Ernie from Moonah

I'd agree with you,
but then we would both be wrong.

April from Wollongong

Keep rolling your eyes . . .
You might eventually find a brain.

Shirley from Turramurra

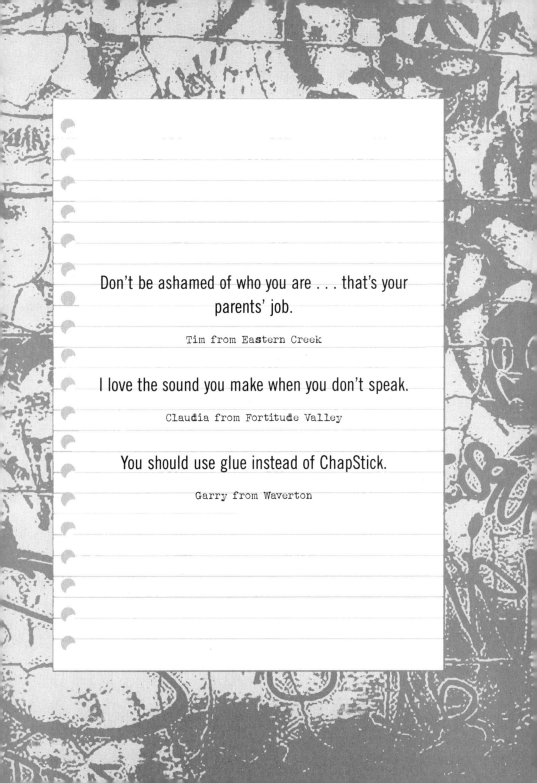

Don't be ashamed of who you are . . . that's your
parents' job.

Tim from Eastern Creek

I love the sound you make when you don't speak.

Claudia from Fortitude Valley

You should use glue instead of ChapStick.

Garry from Waverton

I'll never forget the first time we met
but I'll keep trying.

Alicia from Southport

I've been called worse things by better men.

Tracey from Dundas Valley

You look like you've been drawn with
my left hand from memory.

Jason from St Lucia

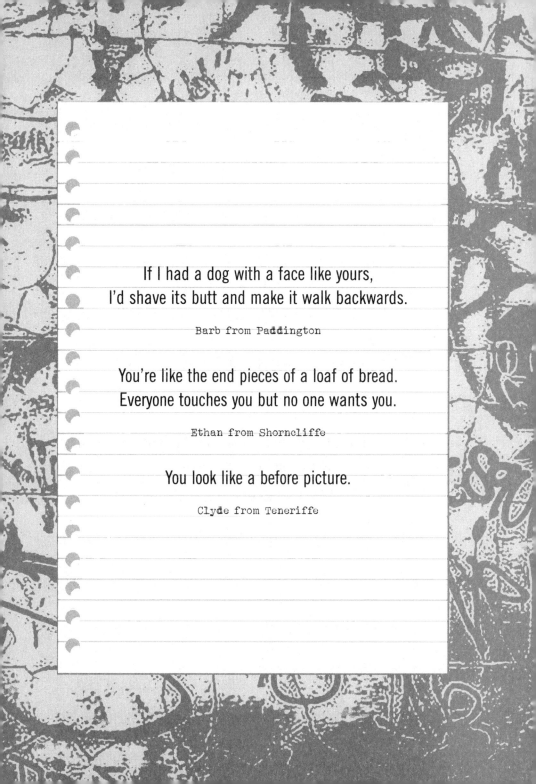

If I had a dog with a face like yours,
I'd shave its butt and make it walk backwards.

Barb from Paddington

You're like the end pieces of a loaf of bread.
Everyone touches you but no one wants you.

Ethan from Shorncliffe

You look like a before picture.

Clyde from Teneriffe

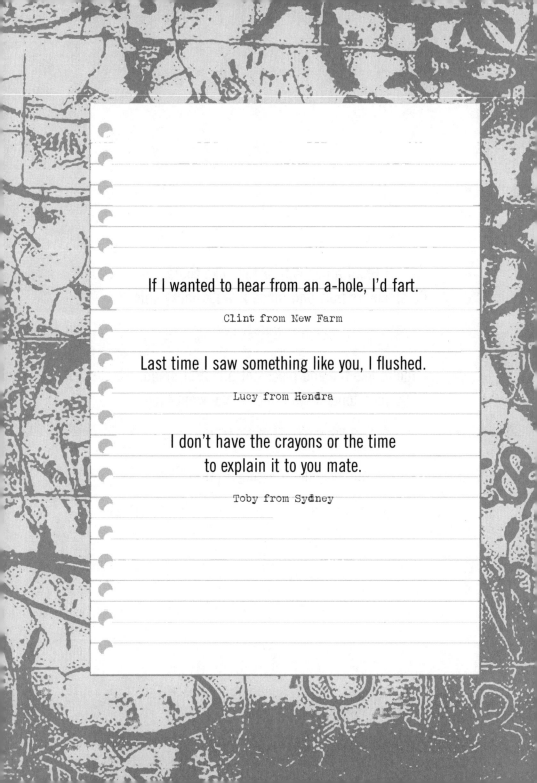

If I wanted to hear from an a-hole, I'd fart.

Clint from New Farm

Last time I saw something like you, I flushed.

Lucy from Hendra

I don't have the crayons or the time
to explain it to you mate.

Toby from Sydney

You're about as useful as a blow-up dart board.

Mathew from Jindalee

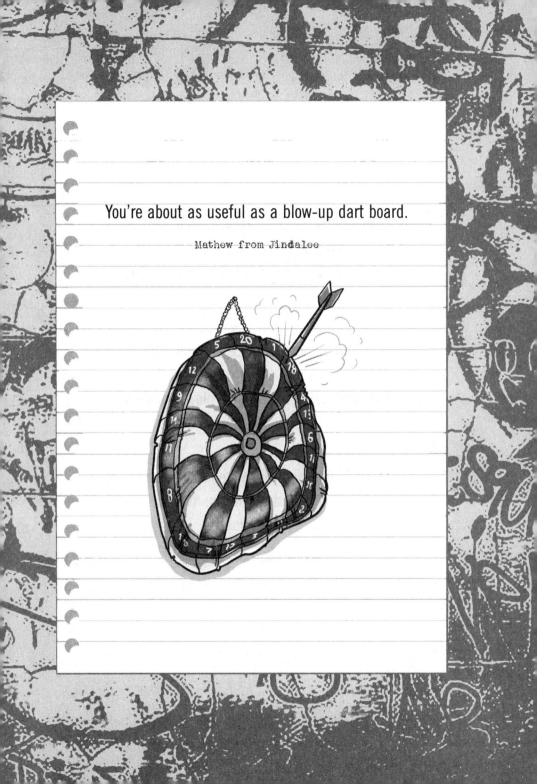

There was a documentary about the clit
released on Netflix, have you seen it?
Yeah I guessed you wouldn't be able to find it.

Mary from Yarra

What's the difference between your
dick and a bonus cheque?
Someone's always willing to blow your bonus.

Leanne from Cranbourne East

You are like a microwave meal. Because you're
finished in two minutes and you look nothing like
your pics.

Leanne from Cranbourne East

Your birth certificate is an apology letter from the condom factory.

Abigail from the Central Coast

You're so ugly, when your mum dropped you off at school, she got a fine for littering.

Carmen from Brisbane

Your family tree must be a cactus, because everyone is a prick.

Renae from Cairns

Someday you'll go far. I hope you stay there.

Greg from Sutherland

Were you born this stupid or did you take lessons?

Emily from Bondi

Learn from your parents' mistakes.
Use a condom.

Rochelle from Coffs Harbour

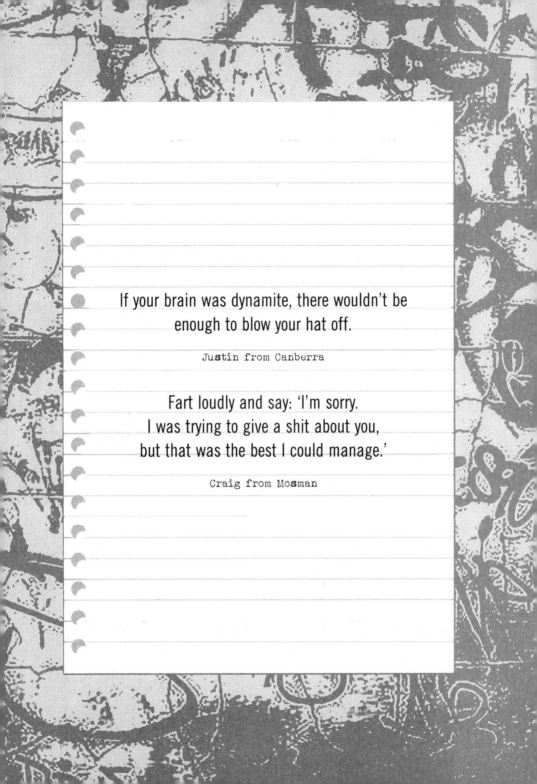

If your brain was dynamite, there wouldn't be enough to blow your hat off.

Justin from Canberra

Fart loudly and say: 'I'm sorry.
I was trying to give a shit about you,
but that was the best I could manage.'

Craig from Mosman

Have you considered hiring a plumber?
It just seems like your verbal filtration system is
letting anything through at this point.

Mill from Brighton

What's the difference between you and a toilet?
Nothing, you're both full of shit.

Leanne from Cranbourne East

CRACKING YARNS

A smorgasbord
of tales

What did you name . . . ? James told us he named his 'tackle' (his penis) Dewey. Intrigued, we asked him why. He said because every time he had to 'do wee', he would whip it out. — **James from Victoria**

A gay man walks into a country bar and says, 'Just to let everyone know, I'm gay, but I won't hit on anyone. I just like country music.' The bartender says it's fine, and the man stays.

The next day the same man comes back with another guy and says, 'This is my brother. I just want everyone to know that we're both gay, but we won't hit on anyone. We just like country music.' The bartender says it's fine and there's nothing to worry about, and the men stay.

The next day the man comes back again. This time he has even more men with him and says, 'These are my cousins and my brother. I just want everyone to know that we're all gay, but we won't hit on anyone. We just like country music.' The bartender says it's really, really, really fine. But he finally gets curious and asks, 'Hey, doesn't *anyone* in your family like women?' The gay man replies, 'Yeah, but she doesn't like country music.' — **Rebecca from Cronulla**

When I was fourteen my dad would cook a lot of lasagne. He once accidentally cooked two massive lasagnes with mincemeat for dogs in them instead of mincemeat for humans, which meant the meat had bits of bone in it that were not meant for people. After going back for seconds and thirds, we realised it was time to feed the dog and there was nothing left for him. Luckily, we spent the rest of the night dry retching while the dog enjoyed a lovely mince lasagne. — **Marcello from Fern Tree Gully**

I was once in a car with my husband, and we drove through a swarm of bees with our windows open. My husband, who was driving, turned to me and said, 'Don't freak out babe, but there are bees everywhere in the car.' He then opened the door of the moving car and jumped out. I stayed in the car as it drove directly into the back of the car in front ... Lucky I didn't freak out when the bees in the car forced my husband to leap from the moving car as he was driving ... Great advice, honey.
— **Nicole from Victoria**

A few years back we were celebrating our end-of-season Mad Monday for the footy club, and we were all dressed up as various characters. This particular year I was dressed as Shrek. I had had a skinful and I needed to go to the bathroom to do a number two so I proceeded to do so. When I finished, I stood up and pulled up the Shrek outfit, not

knowing that half of it had been sitting in the bowl and that's where the poo had landed. So as I put the outfit back on I splattered the poo all over my back, pants and suit, however because I'd had a few drinks I didn't notice, and just walked back out to the party. It wasn't long before the villagers chased this Shrek back to his stinky swamp.
— **Damien from Griffith**

My entire family and all my friends were at my house celebrating the gender reveal of my first child, and we were about to do the reveal on a big screen in front of fifty or so people. My father was in charge of the technology, and when he went to press play we realised that he had obviously accidentally selected some material he might have been watching by himself earlier that day—and so some very detailed porn started playing out loud on the screen in front of everyone. He quickly tried to stop it on his phone and said that it

wasn't porn but in fact yoga tutorials he had been watching online. Everyone was ready to let it go, except his ex-wife (my mother), who yelled out, 'That's the worst excuse I've ever heard, perve!' It was a boy, by the way.
— Jeremy from Mornington

A month ago today, I almost died. I was in my regional farmhouse when a brown snake came up out of nowhere and tried to bite me. To get away from it, I jumped through a glass-panelled window which shattered all around me—remarkably I was uninjured. But then I kept falling and crashed through a second glass panel, which shattered and cut almost every artery in my body, causing me to hit the ground and lose litres of blood within seconds. My partner, who is training to be a nurse, rushed in and kept me alive until the ambulance came and brought me back to life as I felt myself floating off into nothing. If it wasn't for her I would be dead, I have a chronic fear of snakes and spiders . . . and now also glass-panelled windows. — **Jacko from Warringah**

My friend was looking after a dog for her neighbour when it suddenly got sick and died. Panicking, she called me because I am a vet, and I told her to wrap the dog up and bring it into my practice. She put the dead dog into a suitcase and got on the train to come and see me, but en route a man at the station stole the suitcase—with the dead dog inside. She tried to chase him down, but he got away. At least she was able to tell her neighbour that the dog didn't die on her watch, but rather was stolen from her. — **Adele from Brisbane**

I have nicknamed my own son, who is now sixteen, Captain Cockblock. As a single mother I have needs and for some reason when he was growing up he always liked sleeping in the loungeroom when I had friends over, which made it very difficult for me to have special time with people. He now knows I call him this and not only that, all his friends call him Captain Cockblock as well. — **Katy from Brisbane**

I was dating a girl who I thought I was serious with—until I ran into another bloke who said he was dating the same girl. The next day, another guy messaged me and told me he was dating her too. We decided to all meet up at a bar and invite her along. When she rocked up and saw the three of us sitting there, she yelled, 'We have no trust!', bolted, and we never saw her again. The three of us ordered another beer and started playing pool—that was about six years ago, and now the three of us are best mates. — **Dan from Wagga Wagga**

One night out in Melbourne, I went to a gig to see a DJ I liked. I got so fucked up that several hours later I woke up sitting on a plane beside the DJ just as we touched down in Brisbane—I had somehow met him after the show and agreed to go to his next gig on the other side of the country. He paid for the flight, my food and my hotel room and I bendered with him that whole weekend before he paid for my flight home. He is now a pretty famous DJ, and we are best mates. — **Bill from Melbourne**

'What does your name sound like?'
    'Jara.'
    'Okay, sounds fine to us—what's wrong with Jara?'
    'My surname is Dix. So my name is Jara Dix.' — **Jara from Sydney**

FAMOUS PEOPLE FAVES

Jokes and yarns
from our
favourite celebs

GUY SEBASTIAN
singer-songwriter/decent golfer

A man walks into a bar and, to his amazement, he finds a 30-centimetre tall person playing a tiny piano. Stunned, the man asks the bartender where he found this amazing person. The bartender replies that behind the bar is a closet with a genie inside it, who granted him a single wish.

The man dashes into the closet and finds the genie inside. Without hesitation, he wishes for a million bucks, but when he steps out of the closet he sees that one million ducks have suddenly appeared. Infuriated, the man storms through the sea of ducks back to the bartender and screams, 'I think your genie is hard of hearing; I asked for a million bucks but instead I got a million ducks!'

The bartender shakes his head and replies, 'You're telling me . . . Do you really think I asked for a 12-inch pianist?'

MARK CUBAN

businessman/film producer/TV personality

Did you hear about the two antennas that got married?

The wedding was awful, but the reception was amazing.

SAM FISCHER

singer-songwriter/occasional foot model

Say what you want about deaf people . . .

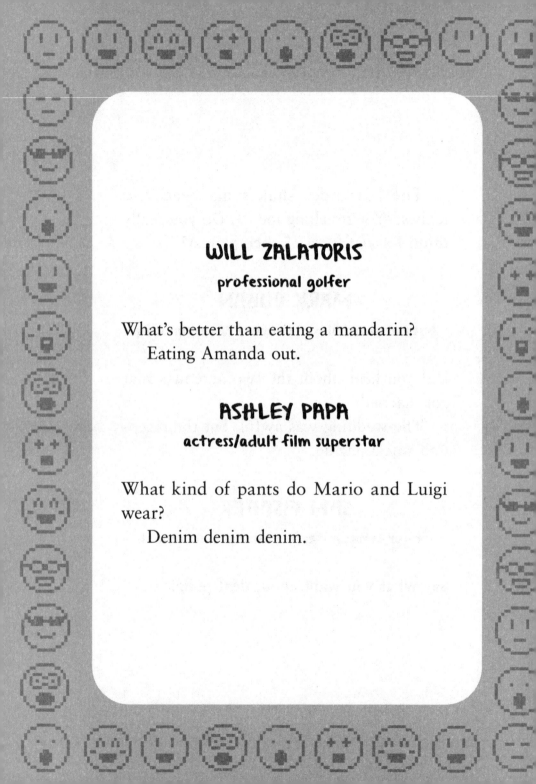

WILL ZALATORIS
professional golfer

What's better than eating a mandarin?
   Eating Amanda out.

ASHLEY PAPA
actress/adult film superstar

What kind of pants do Mario and Luigi wear?
   Denim denim denim.

MARTY AND MICHAEL

comedy duo

What do you call a fish out of water?
A crab.

SAL FROM TWO BROKE CHICKS
podcaster

What do you call friends you like to eat with?

Taste buds.

AL FROM TWO BROKE CHICKS
podcaster

What's the difference between a clit and a golf ball?

A man can find a golf ball.

STINKYASHER

content creator

Did you hear Reese what's-her-name stabbed somebody?
    Witherspoon?
    No, with a knife.

OLLY BOWMAN

content creator

What do you call a guy with no shins?
    Toe-Knee.

GEORGIA McCUDDEN
content creator

If you don't eat you don't shit and if you don't shit you don't die.

JEREMY FRANCO
content creator

Why did Ryan Gosling bring a sandwich to the Oscars?
Because he wanted to win Best Supporting Roll.

ITALIAN BACH

content creator

What do you get when you mix human DNA
with fish DNA?
  Kicked out of the aquarium.

TAMMIN SURSOK

actor/podcast host/presenter

A skeleton walked into a bar and ordered a
beer . . . and a mop.

MARLEE SILVA

presenter/podcast host/in love with Jimmy & Nath

Two nuns are riding their bikes down a cobblestone street on their way to the church.

One nun says to the other, 'I've never come this way before.'

The other nun replies, 'It's probably the cobblestones.'

TILLY ODDY-BLACK
content creator

A man walks into his local pub.

'Hello Donkey,' the barman says. 'Pint of the usual?'

'Yes please,' the man replies.

Another man standing next to him asks, 'Why does he call you Donkey?'

'Hee haw hee haw hee always calls me that.'

MITCHELL COOMBS
content creator/comedian/podcast host

Knock knock.

Who's there?

No one would be knocking for you, you stupid fuck.

SOPHIE McCARTNEY
comedian/author

What happened when the cheese shop exploded?

There was debrie everywhere.

WIL ANDERSON
comedian/author/TV personality/podcast host

What does George Michael like with his stir-fry?

Well, I guess it would be rice.

courtesy of Wil's niece

HARRY GARSIDE
Australian boxer/super-sexy bloke

My girlfriend has started to accuse me of cheating; she's starting to sound like my wife.

JOJO SIWA
singer/dancing sensation

What is Bobo's favourite city?
New Yorky.

EXAMPLE

musician

A man walks into a pub and he goes, 'You lot over there are a bunch of cunts,' and, turning to the other side of the room, 'You guys over there are a bunch of wankers.'

A man stands up and says, 'I'm not a wanker,' and the bloke goes, 'Right, well get over there then, you cunt.'

courtesy of Example's late great-uncle, who was a plumber

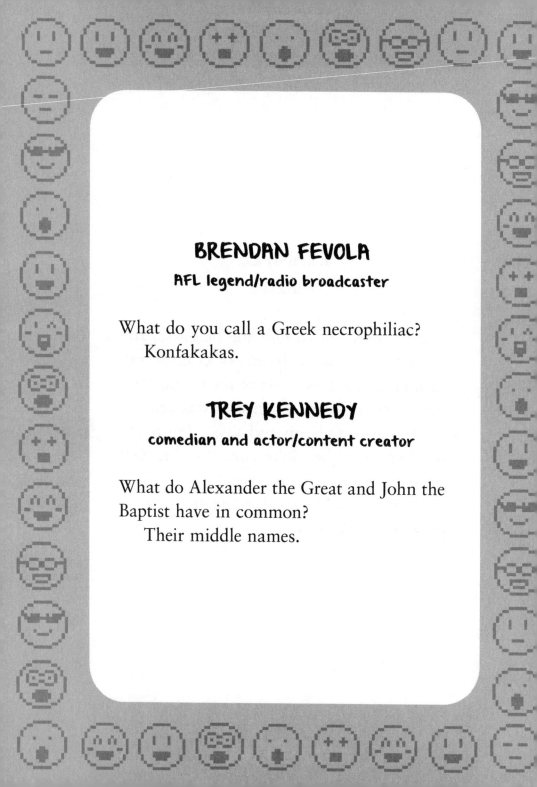

BRENDAN FEVOLA
AFL legend/radio broadcaster

What do you call a Greek necrophiliac?
Konfakakas.

TREY KENNEDY
comedian and actor/content creator

What do Alexander the Great and John the Baptist have in common?
Their middle names.

ARIARNE TITMUS

Olympic swimmer

What do you call it when Batman skips church?
    Christian Bail.

THE VERONICAS

pop duo

So my twin sister called me from prison the other day and said, 'Sooo, you know how we finish each other's sentences . . . ?!'

ASA BUTTERFIELD
actor

What's the difference between an egg and a wank?

You can beat an egg.

MARK GEYER
rugby league legend/radio broadcaster

What's the medical term for Viagra?

Mycoxaflopin.

MACKENZIE ARNOLD
Matildas goalkeeper

What do you call an Italian sex worker?
A pasta-tute.

LUKE AND SASSY SCOTT
podcast hosts/content creators

What do parsley and pubic hair have in common?
You brush them to the side before eating—and they get stuck in your teeth after eating.

STAV DAVIDSON

comedian/broadcaster

Abdul and Mohammed are in detention in Australia. Then a miracle happens and they get their visas granted. As they're leaving detention Abdul says to Mohammed, 'Tell you what—let's meet in front of the Melbourne Cricket Ground one year from today. I bet in one year, I will have become more Australian than you.'

Mo says, 'You're on.'

A year later they meet outside the MCG. Mo pulls up in a Commodore, drinking a VB and smoking a durry, wearing thongs and a trucker singlet. He says, 'G'day Abdul mate. Just dropped the wife at a barbie with the other sheilas, and the kids off at footy practice. What about youse?'

Abdul looks at him and says, 'Fuck off, towel head.'

JULIE GOODWIN

chef/author/presenter

I took my granddaughter to the zoo on the weekend, but it only had one animal, a little dog. It was a Shih Tzu.

GUS WORLAND

radio and TV personality

How many telemarketers does it take to change a lightbulb?

Only one, but he has to do it while you are eating dinner.

MASON COX
AFL player/podcaster

What gets longer when pulled, works best when jerked and inserts into a slot?
    A seatbelt.

SOOSHI MANGO
world-renowned comedy group

My daughter asked me for some personal space, I said alright I will give you personal space with a broom in your face.
    on behalf of Giuseppina

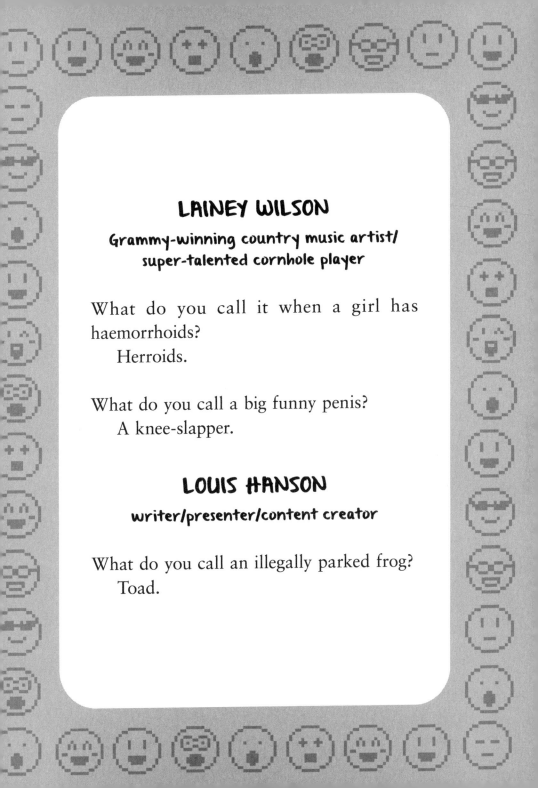

LAINEY WILSON

Grammy-winning country music artist/ super-talented cornhole player

What do you call it when a girl has haemorrhoids?
Herroids.

What do you call a big funny penis?
A knee-slapper.

LOUIS HANSON

writer/presenter/content creator

What do you call an illegally parked frog?
Toad.

TONES AND 1

one of Australia's most streamed artists/ obsessed with Jimmy & Nath

There were three women sitting in a sauna, one older lady and two slightly younger, when suddenly there was a beeping sound. The first young woman pressed her forearm and the beeping stopped. The others looked at her questioningly. 'That was my pager,' she said. 'I have a microchip under the skin of my arm.'

A few minutes later a phone rang, and the second young woman lifted her palm to her ear. When she finished the call she explained: 'That was my mobile phone. I have a microchip implanted in my hand.'

The older woman felt very low-tech. Not to be outdone, she decided to do something just as impressive. She stepped out of the sauna, went to the bathroom and returned with a long piece of toilet paper hanging from her rear end.

The others raised their eyebrows and stared at her.

Finally, the older woman said, 'Well, will you look at that . . . I'm getting a fax.'

TEDDY SWIMS

singer/super-sexy motherfucker

When I came to Australia, I found out that all the koalas had chlamydia . . . Well at least the ones I fucked did.

DASHA
singer/candle thief

Two gay guys are at this bar. One of the guys looks at the other, leans over the bar and says, 'Hey, can I push your stool in?'

LARRY EMDUR
Australian TV personality/presenter

What do you call a sheep that can sing and dance?
   Lady Baba.

MATT SHIRVINGTON
Australian Olympic sprinter/TV presenter

How do you think the unthinkable?
   With an ithberg!

LAST-MINUTE RING-INS

Latecomers and stragglers

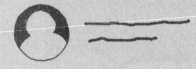

Are you a haunted house?
Because I'm going to scream
when I'm in you.

Kerrod from Rose Bay

Let's play carpenter. First we'll get
hammered, then I'll nail you.

Lauren from Greenwich

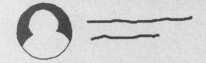

Do you need a stud in your life?
Because I got the STD—all I need is U.

Emily from Penrith

You should sell hot dogs, because you
already know how to make a weiner stand.

Jason from the USA

Maths is easy. First you add the bed,
then you subtract the clothes,
divide the legs and multiply.

Christine from Brisbane

My mate told me he was once
blindfolded and put into a gay porno . . .
He did not know what came over him.

Blake from Maroubra

284

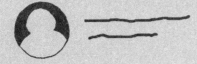

How is a man with a vasectomy
similar to a Christmas tree?
The wood may be hard,
but the balls are purely for decoration.

Chelsea from Blacktown

Why was Boy George banned from the
lizard enclosure?
Because he karma karma cummed
on a chameleon.

Anthony from Kilmore

What do premature ejaculation and hide
and seek have in common?
Ready or not, here I come . . .

Anthony from Kilmore

What's the scariest plant in a forest?
Bam-boo.

Peter from Hoxton Park

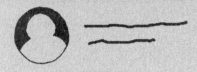

Over the weekend I woke up with a stir-fry all over my bed. I must have been sleep-woking.

Anthony from Kilmore

I went bird-counting with a girl the other day and she was counting the birds real weird. She went, 'Hawk one, and hawk tuah.'

Luke from Fairfield

We call a lady at work Dulux, because she never goes out without two coats on.

Fay from Colorado

Did you hear about the guy who died of a Viagra overdose? They couldn't close his casket.

Rochelle from New Zealand

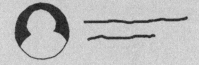

Why does the make-up artist walk funny?
Because her lips stick.

Emily from Ingleburn

What did one lesbian say to the other?
'What's the matter, cat got your tongue?'

Anthony from Kilmore

What do you say to a female soldier you just had sex with?
Thank you for your cervix.

Anthony from Kilmore

We have a guy at work called Rolex—he's easily wound up.

Dave from Amsterdam

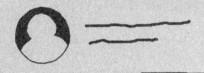

My sister works with someone called Hugh Rae. His nickname is Hip Hip.

Abbey from Miami

Why did David Hasselhoff start going by just the Hoff?
It was 100 per cent less hassle.

Anthony from Kilmore

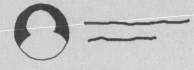

I've got a mate who masturbates with hummus. He is a hummusexual.

Anthony from Kilmore

What brand of shoes do roosters wear?
Ree-bok-bok-bok

Steve from Rouse Hill

Why did the anti-vaxxer's
four-year-old cry?
Mid-life crisis.

Emily from Los Angeles

What's the difference between your mum
and a rooster?
A rooster says cock-a-doodle-do and your
mum says any-cock-will-do.

Mick from Sydney

Three schoolgirls, a redhead, a brunette and a blonde, decide to go to a bar for a drink during schoolies week.

While they're in the bar a policeman walks in and sees them. Being underage, they leave the bar and hide in an old shed at the back of the pub. In the shed there's nothing but empty potato sacks, so the girls decided to hide in them. The policeman sees where they've gone and follows them into the shed.

Looking around, the policeman sees only the potato sacks. He kicks the one with the

redhead hiding inside it, and the redhead yells, 'Meow!'

Must be a cat, thinks the policeman. Then he kicks the second potato sack, the one with the brunette hiding in it. 'Woof woof!' she yells.

Must be a dog, thinks the policeman. He then kicks the third potato sack, the one with the blonde hiding in it, and the blonde yells out, 'Potatoes!'

Brian from Sydney

I saw a group of four teens beating up a little kid so I decided to step in . . . He didn't stand a chance against the five of us.

Anthony from Kilmore

I was at the Olympics and saw a man with a long stick.
I asked him, 'Are you a pole vaulter?'
The man said, 'No I'm German, but how did you know my name?'

Phillip from Sweden

It is illegal to laugh out loud in Hawaii.
Because you need to keep it to a low ha.

Casey from Peakhurst

I found out my girlfriend is really a ghost.
I had my suspicions when she walked
through the door.

Ryan from Parramatta

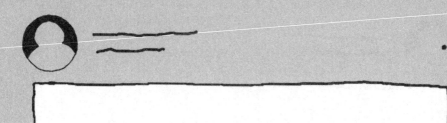

Someone broke into my house and stole all
my fruit. I am peachless.

Eden from Manly

We called our coworker Showbags,
because he was full of shit
and had to be carried.

Mark from Kogarah

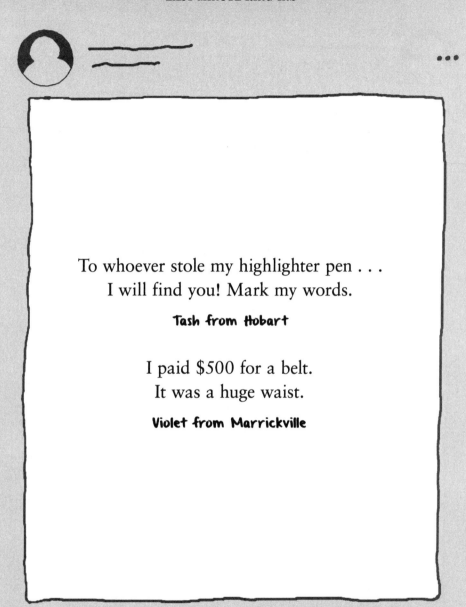

To whoever stole my highlighter pen . . .
I will find you! Mark my words.

Tash from Hobart

I paid $500 for a belt.
It was a huge waist.

Violet from Marrickville

We call a lady at work ET, because all she wants to do is go home.

Stacey from Perth

My girlfriend recently found out I'd been hiding sand and red clay in her food. She shit a brick.

Chris from Loftus

300

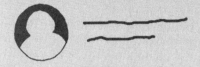

I call a guy in my office 007,
because he has 0 motivation and 0 skills
but he takes 7 shits a day.

Larry from Darwin

We call our trainer Mini Bus,
because he is half a coach.

Emily from Pennant Hills

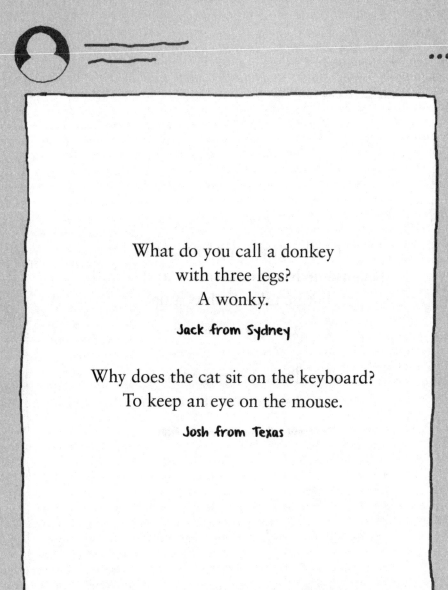

What do you call a donkey
with three legs?
A wonky.

Jack from Sydney

Why does the cat sit on the keyboard?
To keep an eye on the mouse.

Josh from Texas

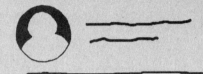

I remember happy times as a youngster
when my dad would roll me down
the hill in a tyre.
Those were Goodyears.

Sam from Russell Lea

What do you call a sheep in a swimsuit?
A lambkini.

Jo from Penrith

303

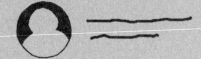

When I was younger, I was walking
down the street and was hit by a violin,
flute and clarinet.
I'm pretty sure it was an
orchestrated attack.

Sam from Russell Lea

How do you know if a blonde's been
using your computer?
There's white-out all over the screen.

Greer from Brooklyn

A FINAL NOTE

Hey guys (and girls), Jimmy & Nath here.

Just wanted to say thank you for reading this book. If you don't listen to our radio show (you should, it's good), you might not know that Jimmy often talks about battling depression and anxiety. Part of the reason we both started doing comedy was to make people laugh.

Life can be fucking hard, and we hope this book will help you forget about that (for a little while). In the meantime, please reach out to someone you know and check on them. Ask them to get a cup of coffee, go for a walk or give them this book when you're done with it. One person, one conversation can make a big difference.

Sometimes laughter isn't enough, so we need you to check in with people too. Because it's nice to know that you don't have to go through life alone.

And if you or someone you know is struggling, please call Lifeline on 13 11 14.

Jimmy & Nath x